"Kevin Regan has produced a creative encore of praying in his new book, *20 More Teen Prayer Services*. The themes (e.g., friendship, competition, sexuality, and heroes) reflect the concerns of adolescents. He provides diverse ways of critically reflecting on relevant issues. These prayer services will challenge adolescents to pray as part of their own way of living. Those who work with adolescents will find this book a valuable asset in teaching them to pray."

Joseph P. Sinwell, D.Min.
Diocesan Director of Religious Education
Diocese of Providence

"Kevin's marvelous new book is outstanding. His exciting activities turn student attention to God in prayer. Moreover, they help build self-esteem, create community, and lead students outside themselves. Kevin is a teacher in touch with the Lord and today's youth. I can't wait to use his prayer services with my own students."

Mike Pennock, Ph.D.
Author, *Friendship in the Lord* high school series

"Adolescents are pray-ers, but they need time, silence, and guidance to develop a deep and lasting relationship with their Creator and Savior.

"Kevin Regan's second book, *20 More Teen Prayer Services,* is a marvelous resource to use with teenagers in encouraging them to pray. The themes of the prayer services will help teenagers to recognize God's action in the experiences of their daily lives."

Brother Daniel F. Casey, F.S.C.
Superintendent of Schools
Diocese of Providence

"*20 More Teen Prayer Services* by Kevin Regan is just what the doctor ordered. So many complain about the situation of our young people. Those who work with them often find them difficult to reach. This volume describes a context in which the religious tradition meets the experience of American teenagers today. Theirs is the experience of school, peer pressure, sex, alcohol, and drugs—all creatively treated here within a context of prayer and thoughtful reflection."

Raymond Collins, Dean
The Catholic University of America

"Kevin Regan has written another book to help youth leaders address challenging topics with teenagers: some new in this culture (gang violence and substance abuse), and some age-old problems (family relationships, boredom). Kevin always focuses on the positive, encouraging teenagers to dream of what they could be, empowering them in their growth.

"No one is ever going to make the teenage years easy; it is a time of exploration and self-identification. But it is critically important for youth leaders to help teens struggle with their issues and make constructive decisions for their lives. Kevin's examples of both women and men, famous and ordinary, help teens identify with their own potential."

Mobby Larson
Author, *Why Can't We Talk?* and *Prayers for Christian Educators*

20 *more* TEEN PRAYER SERVICES

S. KEVIN REGAN

TWENTY-THIRD PUBLICATIONS
Mystic, Connecticut 06355

Twenty-Third Publications
185 Willow Street
P.O. Box 180
Mystic, CT 06355
(203) 536-2611
800-321-0411

ISBN 0-89622-605-4
Library of Congress Catalog Card Number 94-60339
Printed in the U.S.A.

For Linda

Bearer of life, rich in compassion, lover of God's people.
In the gift you offer absolutely, the Absolute is present
with justice and healing, passion and joy.

Contents

Introduction   1

1   **The Courage to Be**   3
    Self-Image and Self-Esteem
        Preparing for Prayer   3
        Prayer Service   5

2   **Sexuality's Power**   7
    Loving and Being Loved
        Preparing for Prayer   7
        Prayer Service   9

3   **Freedom to Dream**   13
    The Challenge of Alcohol and Drugs
        Preparing for Prayer   13
        Prayer Service   15

4   **School**   19
    One Test After Another
        Preparing for Prayer   19
        Prayer Service   21

5   **Friendship**   25
    Together on the Way
        Preparing for Prayer   25
        Prayer Service   27

6   **Daring to Be Me**   31
    Peer Pressure and Conformity
        Preparing for Prayer   31
        Prayer Service   33

7   **Born to Compete**   36
    Winning and Fair Play
        Preparing for Prayer   36
        Prayer Service   38

8   The Cross of Courage   **41**
    Doing What Is Right
        Preparing for Prayer   41
        Prayer Service   43

9   People to Imitate   **45**
    Heroes
        Preparing for Prayer   45
        Prayer Service   48

10 Growing Together   **51**
    Life in the Family
        Preparing for Prayer   51
        Prayer Service   53

11 Called to Be Witnesses   **56**
    The Joy of Being Disciple
        Preparing for Prayer   56
        Prayer Service   58

12 Dare to Dream   **61**
    Vocation
        Preparing for Prayer   61
        Prayer Service   62

13 One With Earth   **65**
    Loving the Planet that Sustains Us
        Preparing for Prayer   65
        Prayer Service   67

14 The Call to Forgive   **70**
    Jesus' Way of Healing
        Preparing for Prayer   70
        Prayer Service   72

15 **Learning Peace**   75
    A Courageous Response to Violence
        Preparing for Prayer   75
        Prayer Service   77

16 **Passion**   80
    A Way Beyond Sex
        Preparing for Prayer   80
        Prayer Service   82

17 **Being With the Poor**   84
    The Way of Justice
        Preparing for Prayer   84
        Prayer Service   86

18 **Human Labor**   88
    More Than Making Money
        Preparing for Prayer   88
        Prayer Service   90

19 **Transformed by God**   92
    Becoming a Eucharistic People
        Preparing for Prayer   92
        Prayer Service   94

20 **Fire in the Belly**   96
    The Dark Night of Adolescence
        Preparing for Prayer   96
        Prayer Service   98

Introduction

Leading adolescents in prayer is a counter-cultural endeavor. The larger society has attempted to eliminate prayer, the spiritual, and a sense of God's mystery from any meaningful place in their lives. The person who would lead the young in prayer experiences is involved in a prophetic activity, challenging the status quo with its propensity toward greed, self-centered indulgence, noise, and contempt for God's poor.

The role of the prophet is to uncover God's abiding presence among us, especially when God appears to be hidden. The role of the prophet is to call us into dialogue with God in prayer and to remind us that we are to love all, including the poor and the broken-hearted who are forgotten and ignored in our consumer-driven society.

Any book intended to help young people pray, especially in group prayer, is part of a challenging endeavor and must address very challenging questions. How do we enter the world of today's youth in a helpful manner? How can we uncover the power of prayer for and with teenagers? How do we help them understand themselves, heal their wounds, and discover the secrets of their deepest longings?

This resource, *20 More Teen Prayer Services*, is meant to help you—youth leaders, clergy, retreat directors, directors of religious education, or teachers—meet these challenges. It is intended to help you prepare reverent, insightful, and prayerful assemblies with teenagers.

It is organized in such a way that it can be used at many different times and in different ways. The prayer services take shape around themes that are central to youth today: peer pressure, self-image, sexuality, athletics, violence, drug abuse, and many others. *Each theme contains two parts: Preparing for Prayer and the Prayer Service itself, and these parts can be used together or separately.*

In some instances it would be most effective to do the Shared Experience on one day and the Prayer Service on a following day. The first part, Preparing for Prayer, contains material needed to help the leader and young people to share common ground around a specific theme. It includes these components:

- •Times for Use suggests a number of feast days or special occasions when the prayer services could be appropriately used.
- •Materials Needed indicates the supplies that will help to develop the theme.
- •The Introduction offers information to stimulate thought about the theme.
- •Shared Experience helps the young people focus on the theme presented.

This first part prepares the teenagers to enter into the prayer service on common ground. Some youth leaders may want to use this section for reflection and stimulus when they prepare their own prayer service or scripture reflection.

The second part, Prayer Service, contains the actual prayer celebration based on a specific theme. Many youth leaders like to work with a small group of young people to prepare the prayer experience. It includes these elements:

- •Focus Prayer is offered to help the group concentrate on the theme and to bond them in their common work. This can also be used independently as opening prayers at assemblies, classes, or retreat gatherings.
- •Through God's Eyes places the theme in the context of God's word in sacred scripture.
- •Reading. It is suggested that the scripture be read from a Bible or from a lectionary, which is the preferred manner of proclaiming it.
- •Quiet Time provides the young people the opportunity to meditate reflectively on God's word addressed to them in the prayer service.
- •The Response invites the adolescents to express themselves—their innermost thoughts and deepest emotions—to God with word and gesture. This opens to the young the life-giving intimacy between God and believer.

Prayer reveals God's loving presence and God's ultimate concern for our well-being. As we pray with the young people entrusted to us, may we be true prophets convinced of God's love for us. May we long for the presence of God wherever love is absent. Above all, may we help those in our care to truly know God's ultimate love and concern for them.

1

The Courage to Be
Self-Image and Self-Esteem

Preparing for Prayer

Times for Use
- beginning or ending a youth appreciation day
- retreat day on the meaning of identity
- confirmation preparation, on discovering oneself
- All Saints Day
- feast of the Baptism of Jesus

Materials Needed
- markers or crayons
- newsprint or plain paper

Introduction

Psychologist Erik Erikson describes the developmental task of adolescence as forming a coherent identity. The ability of young people to enter into intimate relationships depends on their willingness to struggle with this basic task. It is as if each teenager were like Michelangelo trying to envision and free the angel hidden in the marble. The angel in this case is the unique person hidden in the marble of the adolescent's physical, social, intellectual, emotional, and spiritual life.

One goal of this prayer service is to help teenagers not only see their image but recognize its "angelic" qualities. Celebrating their gifts, calling attention to the ways they are responsible, and being with them as an affirming presence are ways to help them discover and value their uniqueness. Centering the celebration in a prayer service helps them see their uniqueness and giftedness as flowing from God's love for them.

Shared Experience
Give each participant a piece of paper and marker. Mention

how important it is to love and accept ourselves. Invite them to think of people they admire because of their confidence, their acceptance of who they are. Explain that although we are all different, we are all loved by God and invited to love ourselves. Then explain: We are going to get in touch with some of our best qualities. This may seem strange because all of us have been taught not to brag. But naming and owning our gifts is not bragging; it is necessary for us to grow in our ability to love.

Ask the young people to think about their best qualities, a particular talent they have. Also, ask them to think of some responsibilities they shoulder that give them a sense of pride. If they say they can't think of any, suggest a few. For example: kindness to friends, caring for a sick relative, visiting an aged grandparent, and athletic or acting abilities.

Next, ask them to draw an outline of their hand or to outline a symbol of how they see themselves. A dancer may draw a ballet slipper, a baseball player a baseball, a loyal friend two rings entwined. Have them write in each finger of the hand (or on their symbol) the ways in which they are responsible, their talents and gifts, or things they do that give them a sense of confidence and pride. They may do this informally with friends at this time or share in groups of three or four. Have them hold on to these images of themselves for a few moments. (Reflective music would be an appropriate accompaniment to the exercise.)

Prayer Service

Focus Prayer

Leader
Loving God, we thank you for making each of us unique in all the world. Some of us are dark-skinned, while others are light. Some of us have curly hair, while others have straight hair. Some of us speak English, while others speak Spanish or Vietnamese as our first language. Some of us are artistic, while others are gifted in math. Some of us are good listeners, while others are gifted athletes. We thank you for making each of us unique.

All
Amen.

Through God's Eyes

Leader
Each of us is a unique, a special person. We are precious because we are created in God's image, and because of the death and resurrection of Jesus, we share a new life in the Spirit characterized by peace and love for all people. No one else can think, feel, or love in the same way we can. Try to see yourselves through God's eyes.

Reading

Reader
This story is about a man who was considered dishonest and was disliked by his neighbors, but Jesus asked him if he could stay at his house. If we realize that God knows us through and through and still loves us completely, it may be easier for us to value and accept ourselves. A reading from the holy gospel according to St. Luke (19:1–10)

Quiet Time
(A few minutes of silence with appropriate soft music)

Leader
The townspeople looked down on Zacchaeus. Perhaps he did not like himself very much because of his job: collecting taxes from his neighbors for Rome, a government that occupied his homeland and was considered an enemy nation. Perhaps, like us, he saw only his failings and shortcomings. But Jesus saw what was in his heart. He wanted Zacchaeus to accept himself and not try to prove his worth by accumulating riches. In the same way, the risen Christ invites each of us to embrace the person we are. Change those things you want to change and

can change, but remember that who we are is more important than what we do. We are—each of us—unique in all the world and loved by God, who comes to stay with us every day of our lives.

Response
(Invite the participants and to come forward one by one, with the drawings they completed earlier. Each will hand the drawing to the leader and name one talent they are proud of. The leader publicly acknowledges the gift and invites the whole community to pray in thanksgiving for the gift of that special person.)

Leader   For Karen's ability to care for her sick grandmother, let us pray in gratitude to God . . .

All   We praise you, Lord, for Karen and her gift.

Leader   (receiving the drawing from the next person) For Michael's skill in playing baseball, let us pray in gratitude . . .

All   We praise you, Lord, for Michael and his gift.

      (Continue until each person has come forward. The drawings are then put in a place of honor, for example, on a table or a wall where they may be viewed by all. If time does not allow each person to present her [his] symbol, ask a representative of each row or group to come forward.)

Leader   Loving God, Jesus often chose to be closest to those others considered sinners, or weak, or unimportant. He comes to stay in our hearts just as he lodged with Zacchaeus. Help us to be open to his presence. Teach us to accept and love ourselves because you love us. And may you who live within bless and empower us to love ourselves in spite of our sins and failings.

All   Amen.

2

Sexuality's Power
Loving and Being Loved

Preparing for Prayer

Times for Use
- retreat day, on "Who am I as a sexual person?"
- ending class work on sexuality and dating
- confirmation preparation, on the meanings and consequences of sexuality
- preparation for a high school prom
- St. Valentine's Day

Materials Needed
- sheets of newsprint and stand
- paper and pencils
- pins
- 2 dummies or dolls, one male and one female

Introduction
Perhaps no single area captures the mind and hearts of teenagers as does sex and sexuality. Their songs, dress, and dating practices often revolve around it. But sexuality is about identity, relationships, and new life. This service illuminates for them the gift of their sexual identity. Through prayer, sexuality will be reverenced as a gift, a source of dignity. It will be celebrated as sacramental, leading the young into the mystery of their own identity, into the mystery of relationships, and into the mystery of union with God. Through this celebration, participants are invited to see sexuality as central to their identity.

Shared Experience
Give each participant a pencil and a piece of paper. Ask: What is the first thing you think about when you hear the words "sex" or "sexual-

ity"? You may get some nervous snickers, since this is such a personal topic. Collect their papers and write their responses on newsprint. Call attention to how sexuality is often associated by young people with problems: AIDS, teen pregnancy, abortion, venereal disease. Explain that these problems are not the result of sex or sexuality but of irresponsible sexual activity. Misusing sex, like misusing any good thing, causes pain and suffering.

Invite the participants to help one another to understand the sexuality of those of the opposite sex. Ask the girls to imagine they are part of a survey for a magazine to discover the ten most common misunderstandings that men have about women. They could each write down five ways they have been misunderstood by boys. Ask the boys to complete the same assignment in regard to the girls. After allowing time for the papers to be completed, ask for volunteers to come forward to read their responses and attach them to the appropriate doll or dummy. If they choose, they may explain why they feel misunderstood. Allow sufficient time for the lively discussion that will ensue. Offer your own reflections on the responsibilities, consequences, and maturity needed to grow into mature sexual people.

Prayer Service

Focus Prayer
(Place 2 lecterns in front of the assembly, with a boy and a girl at each one.)

Girl   Loving God, you have created us as sexual people. Our sexuality is a gift, a power entrusted to us. Through it we are attracted to one another in strong and life-changing ways. Through the physical and emotional longings that accompany our sexuality, you remind us that we are not meant to live in isolation from others. We are created for love.

Boy   Help us to realize the power to love or to destroy that is bound up with our sexual nature. Help us to know that sex is not love, but it can express love.

All   Amen.

Through God's Eyes

Leader   We are influenced by the way we look at things. If we see something as good and precious, we will treat it with respect and value it. If we see something as common and ordinary, we will treat it casually, without much care. This is also true of sexuality. It is truly a precious gift. It is a special way of relating to others and of giving and receiving affection. Sexuality is a mystery that unites our body, mind, and emotions. Sexuality is a complex reality, needing patience and time for all the elements to mature. Society treats this gift, which is complex and profound, as if it were simple and ordinary. No wonder so many people are hurt by their sexuality rather than being energized and made to feel proud of who they are.

        I would like each of you, no matter what your sexual experience, to take time now to reflect on your gift of sexuality and to pray for the guidance and discipline necessary to use the gift maturely and responsibly.

Reading

Reader   There are many references to sexuality in the Bible. I would like to read one account now, in which the creation of Adam and Eve as sexual beings is described. A reading from the book of Genesis (2:21–25)

Reprinted with permission from *20 More Teen Prayer Services* by Kevin Regan
© 1994 Twenty-Third Publications, P.O. Box 180, Mystic, CT 06355. 800-321-0411

Quiet Time
(A few mintes of silence with appropriate soft music)

Leader   If we listen carefully, we see that we are male and female, created in the image of God. That is what sexuality is about, our identity, who we are. God also told the couple to increase and multiply. So sexuality is also about fruitfulness. Pregnancy, often seen as a problem and something unwanted, is meant to be a desired outcome of sexual love. Sexuality is also about intimacy, about people drawing close to each other in responsible and caring ways. God looks upon our sexuality as good.

No matter how we have behaved sexually up until now, we can begin anew to see sexuality from God's perspective. Let us learn to know ourselves and love ourselves before seeking sexual intimacy with others. Let us learn that there are different ways of sharing affection, not only genital expression. Let us help one another to value sexuality by treating one another with respect, and never leading others into irresponsible sexual activity.

Response

Leader   We will now pray three litanies. During the prayer of petition, ask God for the gifts you may need regarding your sexuality. During the prayer for forgiveness, feel free to mention something for which you want to be forgiven. Finally, during the prayer of gratitude, you may mention some aspect of your sexuality you are thankful for. (If desired, you may prepare these prayers with a smaller group of young people before the service begins. These people will then read these prayers during the service.)

Litany of Petition
(Response: Loving God, hear our prayer.)

Leader   Let us pray, remembering we are in the presence of God. God, you created man and woman in your own image, male and female. Hear our prayer as we seek your help, ask your forgiveness for our failings and sins, and express our gratitude for your gifts. For the ability to love ourselves and learn to treasure our sexual identity, let us pray to the Lord . . .

All   Loving God, hear our prayer.
(If a teenager leads each prayer, after the reading, have her

[him] take the prayer and place it in a receptacle on the altar or on a table in front of the assembly. He [she] should then stand around the table until the end of the service.)

Leader	That we may always act responsibly as sexual persons, remembering the difference between sex and love, let us pray to the Lord . . .
All	Loving God, hear our prayer.
Leader	That we may be aware of the non-genital ways of showing affection, let us pray to the Lord . . .
All	Loving God, hear our prayer.
Leader	I invite you now to mention any special needs for which you would like to pray.
All	Loving God, hear our prayer. (As often as needed)

Litany of Forgiveness
(Response: Jesus our Savior, forgive us.)

Leader	We now pray for God's forgiveness for our sins and failures. For the times we have selfishly used another person made in God's image, let us pray to the Lord . . .
All	Jesus our Savior, forgive us.
Leader	For the times we have failed to accept the consequences of our sexual activity on the lives of other people, let us pray to the Lord . . .
All	Jesus our Savior, forgive us.
Leader	For the times we have failed to help others to know and value their sexuality, we pray to the Lord . . .
All	Jesus our Savior, forgive us.
Leader	I now invite you to mention those things for which you need God's forgiveness.
All	Jesus our Savior, forgive us. (As often as needed)

Litany of Thanksgiving
(Response: Holy Spirit, we thank you for your gifts.)

Leader   Let us now thank God for the gift of sexuality, for the gift of being female or male, people created in God's image and likeness, let us pray to the Lord . . .

All   Holy Spirit, we thank you for your gifts.

Leader   For the gift of friendships and being able to give and receive affection, we pray to the Lord . . .

All   Holy Spirit, we thank you for your gifts.

Leader   For the ability to experience intimacy and to pass on the gift of new life, we pray to the Lord . . .

All   Holy Spirit, we thank you for your gifts.

Leader   I invite you to mention any aspect of your sexuality for which you would like to thank God.

All   Holy Spirit, we thank you for your gifts. (As often as needed)

Leader   (Invite all gathered to join hands as a sign of affection. You join hands with those gathered around the altar and say) We offer you, God, the gift of our sexuality. We pledge to use its power for compassion, healing, and love. All join me in responding.

All   We pledge to use the power of our sexuality only for love.

              (Invite the teenagers to silently ask God's blessing on the person on their right and then on their left with special gifts such as peace, generosity, and joy. When all have had time to do this, ask each person to say so long to those next to them with some sign of peace.)

3

Freedom to Dream
The Challenge of Alcohol and Drugs

Preparing for Prayer

Times for Use
- before a prom or high school graduation
- before final exams
- before holidays or vacations
- confirmation preparation, on freedom
- part of a day on vocations
- St. Patrick's Day
- Pentecost

Materials Needed
- empty beer cans or liquor bottles, empty pill bottles
- pictures of young people happily working and playing together
- markers and a piece of paper for each participant
- 4 candles
- the words "My Dream" on a board or large sheet

Introduction

Every day, 1000 teenagers ages 10–14 start drinking alcohol and more than 500 begin using illegal drugs. The harmful consequences of alcohol and drug use among these young people are familiar to all: dropping out of school, loss of friends, inability to hold a job, and even death.

One of the deepest longings of most adolescents is to be free, independent. This prayer service will look at freedom in relation to their dreams for the future. It will challenge them to consider what effects alcohol and drug use will have on their freedom, their dream. It will celebrate the dignity of the person who is truly free.

Shared Experience

Give each participant a marker and a piece of paper. Call attention to the pictures of young people working and laughing and to the words, "My Dream." Ask them to consider what dream they have for themselves. Give them some help starting. You may name your dream when you were their age, or list some dreams such as becoming a great musician, working with children as a teacher or doctor, becoming an actor or an astronaut. Ask them to draw a symbol of their dream on the right side of the paper. For example, a test tube could symbolize a scientist, a sneaker could symbolize a professional athlete, and a guitar could symbolize a musician. After each person has had the opportunity to draw a symbol of their dream, ask volunteers to share what they have drawn. Next, ask each one to draw a symbol of himself (herself) on the left side. Stick figures may be used.

Call attention to the whiskey and beer bottles and the pill bottles. Ask each person to draw a bottle on the paper between their dream and the symbol of himself and herself. Ask how drinking or using drugs would affect their chances of reaching their dream. You can use this time to explain the attraction and dangers of alcohol and drug use or give some examples of dreams that have been lost to alcohol or drug use. Direct the young people to hold on to their papers.

Prayer Service

Focus Prayer

Leader   We are gathered in prayer to reflect on our dreams, the freedom we need to make them a reality, and the danger of alcohol and drugs coming between us and our dreams.

Pray-er 1   (moving beside the Leader) Lord, you are my friend. Help me to know my dream, accompany me on my journey as I try to make it happen. Help me to have the freedom to overcome the obstacles that will separate me from my dream. Help all those who find it difficult to say no to alcohol and drugs.

All   Amen.

Through God's Eyes

Leader   I wonder if God has a dream for us. I believe God does. I find this dream most clearly expressed in the words and works of the man Jesus. When I read of Jesus healing a sick person, I understand God's dream, and I know that God inspires all who dream of being healers as nurses, doctors, chiropractors, and technicians. When I hear how Jesus fed the hungry, I know God's dream for us. I also understand that God inspires people to be farmers, chefs, as well as political and religious leaders who work to ensure that all people receive enough food to live with dignity. When I realize that Jesus' best friends were fishermen, I realize the dignity of those who dream of working on ships or of finding new ways of replenishing our oceans with fish. Jesus was a teacher, a carpenter's son, the child of a loving mother. Through his life on Earth, God blessed all those who dream.

I also wonder what God thinks of the many young people who surrender their dreams and their freedom to the power of alcohol and drugs. Today many don't know how to have a good time without drink. Many use it as a way of handling stress or escaping from problems. God must be perplexed at the number of young people who demand freedom from their parents but surrender their freedom and their consciousness to the power of chemicals. As we listen to God's word, let us reflect on our dreams and the freedom we will need to make decisions to make them reality.

Reading

Reader   I would like to read one description of God's dream for us. This parable tells of the surprise of the just when they discover what they did to the smallest they did to God. The damned are equally surprised to find that in neglecting the "least" person they neglected Christ. A reading from the holy gospel according to Matthew (25:31–46)

Quiet Time
(A few minutes of silence with appropriate soft music)

Leader   "I have a dream," said Martin Luther King, Jr. and by speaking out, writing, marching, praying, going to jail, and finally dying, he worked to make his dream a reality. Dorothy Day and Peter Maurin had a dream of a society where it would be easier for people to do good and love one another than to do evil. Together they founded the Catholic Worker Movement to feed, clothe, and shelter God's poor and to build a nonviolent society. Fr. Bruce Ritter had a dream that every runaway teenager would have a place of safety to go to in times of crisis. He founded Covenant House in New York City and in cities throughout the world. Maura Clark, Ita Ford, Dorothy Kinsel, and Jean Donovan had a dream that orphans in the war-torn country of El Salvador would be cared for. They gave their lives to make that dream a reality. People as different as Mother Teresa and Jackie Robinson or Albert Einstein and Erma Bombeck have made their dreams reality by making tough decisions that supported their goals, their dreams. The decision to drink or do drugs would have defeated their hopes and dreams just as it destroys the dreams of many young people today. Let us join in prayer to ask God to help us to the freedom we need to arrive at our dream.

Response
(Place 5 lecterns in front of the assembly. Place 4 lighted candles, a beer bottle, and a pill bottle on the altar or on a table in front of the assembly.)

Leader   Loving God, your Holy Spirit is a spirit of freedom, of creativity, of dreams and imagination. Help us to resist the temptation to give away our freedom to the power of alcohol and drugs. Who will speak for God's Spirit on our behalf?

Pray-er 1	God, you created us free but there are many forces that would take away our freedom. It is hard, Lord, not to drink at parties, after a dance or a ballgame. It is hard, Lord, to handle the stress of school, parents, work, relationships, and planning for the future. It is hard to just say no. Help us, Holy Spirit, spirit of freedom. All join me in praying to God's Spirit . . .
All	Help us, Holy Spirit, spirit of freedom. (Pray-er 1 takes a lighted candle and holds it.)
Pray-er 2	Loving God, we are influenced by our friends and society. Give us friends who will help us to make good decisions and influence us to choose the light of freedom over the slavery of drugs. Let us all pray together . . .
All	Help us, Holy Spirit, spirit of freedom. (Pray-er 2 takes a lighted candle.)
Pray-er 3	Holy Spirit, give us the courage to say no to what destroys our dreams and to begin now to take steps to make our dreams reality. Let us pray together . . .
All	Help us, Holy Spirit, spirit of freedom. (Pray-er 3 takes a lighted candle.)
Leader	Loving God, your son, Jesus, invited us to make his dream our dream. Who will speak on our behalf to Jesus, our brother and friend?
Pray-er 4	Jesus, you know our struggle because you lived it. You know how hard it is to choose what is good. You know how lonely it can be to do the right thing. You know that alcohol and drugs appear to us as something that will help us or make us happy while all the time they are destroying us by enslaving us to their chemical reactions. Give us the grace, the presence, to recognize the evil behind the pretended good. Jesus, may each of our dreams become a part of your dream for the freedom and dignity of each person. All join in affirming our belief in the dream of Jesus . . .
All	Help us, Holy Spirit, spirit of freedom. (Pray-er 4 takes a candle.)
Leader	(raising hands in blessing) Go with the freedom of God's chil-

dren, a freedom to love, not hate, to make peace, not violence, to create comfort, not sorrow, and a freedom from the slavery of alcohol, drugs, and every force that would take away your dignity as God's children. I invite you to affirm God's blessing by saying Amen, Amen.

All   Amen, Amen.

(If the assembly is small enough, a candle may be given to each participant as a reminder of the choice for freedom that is always present.)

4

School
One Test After Another

Preparing for Prayer

Times for Use
• opening of school year
• conclusion of a quarter or a semester
• retreat day on the meaning of education
• part of confirmation preparation, on the gifts of wisdom and
  knowledge
• patron saint of your school
• feast of St. John Baptist de LaSalle, patron saint of teachers
• feast of St. Dominic or St. Thomas Aquinas

Materials Needed
• pencils
• an outline of a school building, with no windows or doors
• 1 or 2 markers
• 2 sheets of newsprint
• chalkboard

Introduction
Education means to lead or draw out, and "school" comes
from the Latin *schola*, which means learned leisure. Education in a school set-
ting might mean the leading of a young person out of childhood and adolescence in the surroundings where learning is a leisurely process, where
learning to relate to leisure can take place. Education can also mean drawing
out from the child the gifts and talents hidden within. One wonders if education today has any resemblance to these images. Students see school as
one test after another because education has become cut off from their own
personal mystery, the unfolding of their life in God. When the primary goal
of education is getting a job or socialization, it is robbed of its depth, its adventure, and its dynamism. This prayer service hopes to locate education at

the center of a process of self-discovery where the ability to reason is united to the ability to love and relate. The source and end of this continuous unfolding is the God of life who spoke the perfect word for our education in the person of Jesus.

Shared Experience

Give each participant a pencil and piece of paper. Invite them to think about school. Specifically, ask them to describe their experience of school, what it is like to go to school five days a week. Second, ask them to explain the purpose of school. Give them time to think about their responses, and then ask them to complete the outlined school building by drawing in rooms that symbolize what their experience of school is and what purpose school has for them. Someone may draw a "boring room" with people sleeping in it to illustrate their experience of school. Another room might be all gym, or the music room, to illustrate school as they see it. You may have such a school outlined on half of the chalkboard with their suggestions. Give them time to complete their artwork. Afterward, invite them to share their responses. Allow time for discussion.

On the reverse side of the paper have the participants name a gift or talent they would like to develop through education. The ability to think, to solve problems, to understand science or math, to develop artistic skills are a few examples. Draw a second school on the other half of the blackboard and fill the rooms with these abilities.

Prayer Service

Focus Prayer

Leader   Jesus, you invited us to address God as our loving father. But today we want to pray to you as our teacher and ask you to help us to understand more fully the meaning of education. Often school seems like one test after another. It all seems so boring or worthless. Help us today to discover new ways to think about school and education. Help us to become involved learners like your apostles. Help us to see education as an adventure, discovering who we are, who you are, and the most loving ways to use our talents. We pray this on behalf of all those who "sit in the back of the class."

All   Amen.

Through God's Eyes

Leader   We have gathered to reflect and to pray. We reflect on our experience of school and education, on what education has come to mean to many of us. We pray that we may see that our education is not something apart from us. It is not something someone else can give to us. Our education is ours only if we make it our own. Only by applying the skills we develop to our own lives and place in our world will our education become truly our own. By seeing school as part of the process of education, of self-discovery, we come to realize that our education is a life-long discovery not only of ourselves and others and our world but of God. Let's listen to one way God may be inviting us to see our own education.

Reading

Reader   St. Paul writes that the believers may know Christ through faith and may be rooted in love. He further hopes they may know the expanse of Christ's love, that they be filled with the fullness of God. A reading from the letter to the Ephesians (3:14–19)

Quiet Time

(A few minutes of silence with appropriate soft music)

Leader   How are Paul's words connected to education, to your education? A story will illustrate.

Reprinted with permission from *20 More Teen Prayer Services* by Kevin Regan
© 1994 Twenty-Third Publications, P.O. Box 180, Mystic, CT 06355. 800-321-0411

Once a small child asked a doctor what motivated her to study so hard and for so many years. The doctor said she wanted to be wealthy. The child received this explanation with disappointment and moved on. Next the child met a great actor. The child asked how he could spend so many hours studying and memorizing lines and rehearsing hour after hour. The actor proudly boasted that he longed to be famous. Again the child moved on in disappointment. Next the child met the chief executive officer of an international corporation. The child asked how he could work so hard, attend many meetings, and travel so much. The C.E.O. replied that being in charge gave him a sense of power and immortality. Once again the child moved on in disappointment.

Finally, the child met a woman caring for babies who had AIDS. She wasn't paid much for her work and the hours and labor were demanding. Why would she work unnoticed, taking care of babies with AIDS? the child inquired. Surely she could use her medical training to make more money in other ways. The woman paused, looked lovingly at the baby in her arms and said, "I realize, holding these babies, that God has given me many gifts. I want to love in return." The child looked around at the babies and realized the wisdom in the woman's words: "I want to love in return." This woman was filled with the love of Christ, and this surpasses knowledge. Education, for her, was not about what she needed or what she could get from her schooling. It had to do with the kind of person she had become, what she could give to others.

Response
(Have the chalkboard in front of the assembly with the two schools drawn on it. One has written over it, "One test after another." The other with the talents of the teenagers listed has written over it, "A way to love in return.")

Leader   We will respond to God's presence by expressing our needs, hopes, and gratitude. You are the center of our learning activities, so I will count on you to respond. Think first of one thing you should do in relation to your schoolwork; for example, working harder in school, or building a better relationship with a certain teacher. (Pause to allow students to think of the needs they have. Ask for three volunteers who will present their needs as representatives of the group.)

Next, think of some hopes you have for your future. What

are some of the ways you hope to develop your gifts and use them in the world? (Allow them to write down their hopes. They may use the hopes they listed in the shared experience for this. Ask for three or four volunteers to present their hopes.)

Finally, think of your gifts, the talents you have, the things you do well. (Pause for them to think of talents they are thankful for. Ask for three or four volunteers to present their talents in thanksgiving to God.)

Prayer of Petition

Leader   Loving God, school is sometimes boring but it is meant to be a challenge, an adventure in self-discovery. Hear us as we use our gifts to ask your help to be better students. I invite those people who have come forward with needs to lead us in prayer. Our response will be, Loving God, be with us at school. (The following prayers are provided as a supplement to, not a substitute for, the prayers of the teenagers.)

Pray-er 1   For our need to become more involved in our education, we ask God to hear us . . .

All   Loving God, be with us at school.

Pray-er 2   For the ability to concentrate and study and complete homework, we ask God to hear us . . .

All   Loving God, be with us at school.

Pray-er 3   For a better relationship to my teachers and more enthusiasm about my work, we ask God to hear us . . .

All   Loving God, be with us at school.

Prayer of Hope

Leader   God of hope, you helped Jesus to grow and mature and to be educated as a boy of his time. Hear us as we place our hopes for a good education in your care for us. Our response will be, God of hope, help us to grow.

Pray-er 1   Lord, we hope that our gifts and talents will be needed and respected by our society. Hear us, Lord of hope . . .

All	God of hope, help us to grow.
Pray-er 2	God, Jesus grew in wisdom and knowledge. Help us to know our gifts and to grow in both wisdom and knowledge. Hear us, God of hope . . .
All	God of hope, help us to grow.
Pray-er 3	We are often fearful for our futures for we live in an insecure world. Give us hope in the future because you are a faithful and loving God.
All	God of hope, help us to grow.

Prayer of Thanksgiving

Leader	Loving God, you have blessed each of us with many beautiful gifts and talents. Hear us as we thank you for your blessings on us. Our response will be, We want to love in return.
Pray-er 1	For the ability to think and solve problems and make our own decisions, we thank the Lord . . .
All	We want to love in return.
Pray-er 2	For the gift of health and for athletic ability, we thank the Lord . . .
All	We want to love in return.
Pray-er 3	For the ability to love and to use our education for the good of others, we thank the Lord . . .
All	We want to love in return.
Leader	Lord of all learning, we pray to you to help us understand that our education is about who we are and how we relate to you, to others, and to Earth. Help us to take our education seriously and to use it, like the woman in the story, to love you in return for your love. We pray this in Christ's name.
All	Amen.

5

Friendship
Together on the Way

Preparing for Prayer

Times for Use
• youth recognition night
• retreat day focusing on relationships
• confirmation preparation, on the gift of God's friendship
• feast of St. Francis, friend of all God's creatures

Materials Needed
• yarn
• paper
• pencils
• pictures of friends

Introduction
Friendship is clearly a primary concern of most adolescents. As they move away from dependence on parents toward the independence of adults, friends often supply the companionship, guidance, and solace once sought mainly in the home. Friends are given priority, whether at the other end of a phone line or on the other side of the classroom. Their influence for better or worse can have lasting consequences. The quality of one's character and the direction of one's life bear the imprint of the friends one chooses. This service celebrates God's presence through the gift of friends.

Shared Experience
Invite the teenagers to take out pictures of their friends and allow time for them to share stories and memories with each other. (These pictures could have been placed around the room beforehand.) As they look at their pictures, indicate that this exercise and prayer service will focus on the importance of friendship. Give each participant a pencil and piece of loose-

leaf paper and ask them to list two or three problems they are having right now. They need not sign the papers. Problems may be in school, in relationships, with family, or other areas of concern. Ask them to think of how difficult it is to try to carry problems or burdens alone.

Next, have the young people break into groups of about ten to twelve people and form circles. Give one person in each group a large ball of yarn. This person tosses the ball of yarn to another person in the group. Continue this until a web is formed. Then ask one member of the group to take the pieces of paper with the burdens written on them and spread them on top of the web. Use this exercise to help the young people explore the importance of friendship in their lives. You might highlight the ability of friends to help ease our burdens in time of conflict or confusion. Allow time for them to share some of their observations on friendship's importance. Point out that qualities such as loyalty, forgiveness, honesty, and humor are all a part of being a friend. Having someone to stand by us in time of need is one of life's great gifts.

(If the young people know each other well, they could name one quality of friendship possessed by the person to whom they throw the yarn.)

Prayer Service

Focus Prayer

Leader Let us pray for one another, that we may know our friends and value their presence through life. I pray that what we say and do here may help each of us to be more grateful for our friends. Help us, loving God, never to take our friends for granted, and help us to know that you love us through our friends.

All Amen.

Through God's Eyes

Leader Just think how lonely our journey through life would be if we never had friends. They help us to enjoy good times more, and diminish the pain of the bad times. With our friends we can really be ourselves and accept our weaknesses. They teach us that we are valuable just the way we are. Maybe this is one reason Jesus called his followers friends. He showed them and us that no matter how we fail by our sins, God is always there for us.

If some of us have difficulty making friends, we may find the following story helpful. In it we see the beauty and power of friendship to heal wounds and give life. We also realize true friendship demands sacrifice from us.

Reading

Reader I want to share with you the story of Naomi and Ruth. Naomi tells her daughters-in-law to find husbands for themselves. Ruth refuses to leave her widowed mother-in-law, and goes with her to a strange land. The beautiful fidelity of Ruth toward Naomi is described in the reading, a wonderful example of God's fidelity and friendship. A reading from the book of Ruth (1:8–18)

Quiet Time

(A few minutes of silence with appropriate soft music)

Leader What a wonderful example of friendship Naomi and Ruth give us. Loyalty, generosity, being there in time of need, sharing a friend's sorrow and joy—all the ingredients of friendship are here. Perhaps we don't value our friends as we should. It was when Naomi was alone and in mourning that she felt most deeply the gift of Ruth's friendship. We reveal what is most precious and most vulnerable within us to our closest friends. They know us inside out.

Let us now think of our friends with deep gratitude. We recognize them as wonderful gifts, and in them we can also recognize the love of God. Jesus told his closest followers that they were not his servants but friends to whom he had opened his heart. It is right that we celebrate our friends, and that we thank God for the gift of friendship.

Response

Leader   (Invite those gathered to form 5 circles, one within the other [or use 2 or 3 circles, as circumstances suggest]. The first circle may have 5 people, the second, 8, etc. Have 1 youth leader in each circle. When everyone is in place, you say:) Let us help one another to celebrate our friendships and thank God for giving us people who are there for us on life's journey.

Youth
Leader   (from innermost circle) I invite all in this circle to join hands as a sign of the unity friendship creates. Let each person in this circle say the first name of one friend and we will all respond, Lord, we praise you for the gift of our friend.

Speaker 1   For John . . .

All   Lord, we praise you for the gift of our friend.

Speaker 2   For Marita . . .

All   Lord, we praise you for the gift of our friend.

Youth
Leader   (in second circle) Let us join hands also in the name of friendship and thank God for the special gifts our friends bring us. Each person is invited to name one gift and we will all respond: We thank you, Lord.

Youth
Leader   For the gift of laughter and the good times my friend brings me, let us pray to the Lord . . .

All   We thank you, Lord.

Speaker 1	(in second circle) For the gift of helping me to accept and love myself, let us pray to the Lord.
All	We thank you, Lord.
Speaker 2	(in second circle) For the gift of being there during my toughest moments, let us pray to the Lord.
All	We thank you, Lord.
Youth Leader	(in third circle) We, too, join hands, for friendship has helped us to overcome loneliness and brought us the company of one who cares for us. Let us pray for the needs of our friends and for those who do not have any friends. Our response will be: Jesus our friend, hear our prayer.
Youth Leader	When our friends are lonely, let them know we care, for this we pray to the Lord of friendship . . .
All	Jesus our friend, hear our prayer.
Speaker 1	(in third circle) For friends who are addicted to drugs or alcohol, let us pray to the Lord of friendship . . .
All	Jesus our friend, hear our prayer.
Speaker 2	(in third circle) For friends who are afraid and hide behind masks, let us pray to the Lord of friendship . . .
All	Jesus our friend, hear our prayer.
Speaker 3	(in third circle) For those who are alone and seek the gift of a friend, let us pray to the Lord of friendship . . .
All	Jesus our friend, hear our prayer.
Youth Leader	(in fourth circle) We, too, join hands as a sign that problems and worries are a burden to carry alone, but friendship can make them lighter. The response to my prayers will be: Jesus, grant us the gift of friendship.

Youth Leader	When we feel alone, as if no one cares we pray to the Lord . . .
All	Jesus, grant us the gift of friendship.
Youth Leader	When we have a secret so heavy and painful we think no one will understand or care, let us pray to the Lord . . .
All	Jesus, grant us the gift of friendship.
Youth Leader	When others are alone and need our care and our compassion, let us pray to the Lord . . .
All	Jesus, grant us the gift of friendship.
Leader	Loving God, you have given us friendship as one of your most precious gifts and one of the greatest signs of your presence with us. Bless each person here and let them know the joy and peace that results from having lasting and loyal friends. We pray this in the name of Jesus our friend.
All	Amen.
Leader	Let us close our celebration by offering each other a sign of peace.

6

Daring to Be Me
Peer Pressure and Conformity

Preparing for Prayer

Times for Use
- new school year
- before prom
- freshmen or sophomore retreat program
- career day for seniors in high school
- confirmation preparation, on courage
- vocation awareness day
- feast of St. Thomas More

Materials Needed
- pencils
- questions on sheet of paper
  1. Can I make decisions on my own?
  2. Do I crave attention?
  3. Am I driven to be popular?
  4. Do I have a set of values to guide me in life?
  5. What are my values concerning alcohol and drugs, dating, the use of violence to solve conflict?
  6. Am I my own best friend?

Introduction
Adolescence is a time of gathering new information, new experiences, new emotions, new thinking powers, and new questions about identity. This all helps form their developing identity and world view. At this time, a time of transition, friends and peers often replace parents as the main source of authority. Physical, emotional, and social changes in the adolescent make the opinion of peers important in the extreme. This prayer

service recognizes the tension between wanting to fit in and conform, and wanting to be true to self. It seeks to help teenagers acknowledge the reality of peer pressure and to feel empowered to overcome it by knowing their gifts and the cost of conformity.

Shared Experience

Pass out the pencils and the sheet of questions to each participant. Explain that this prayer service will focus on the difficulty of being ourselves in a world that constantly invites us to conform to its standards. Ask them to think about peer pressure in their lives, and to answer the questions provided. Then ask if they see any connections between the questions asked and the ability to resist peer pressure. Let them discuss specific questions. Point out that we become our true selves by choosing our own set of guidelines and values, by loving and trusting ourselves enough so that we don't depend on the approval of others to feel good about ourselves. End by asking the participants whether they are free enough from peer pressure to choose to become the person they want to be, or are they led into a future not of their choosing.

Prayer Service

Focus Prayer

Leader We pray to God who created us to be a free people. We pray to God who loves us with a motherly love that we might be unique and return love as only we can. We pray to the Spirit of God who gives us the courage to be ourselves, especially when others are leading us away from our values and the truth as we know it.

Through God's Eyes

Leader Sometimes we may feel that God does not hear us or even abandons us in the time of deepest need. When we are at a party and being pressured to go along with the crowd or when on a date and we think "everyone is doing it," we may find it hard to say no to the crowd and to do what we think is right. God is present and our conscience reminds us of the right thing to do, to hold on to our values, even when it is tough to do so. Listen to this reading from holy scripture about a beautiful Jewish girl who was willing to accept death rather than betray her conscience and God.

Reading

Reader 1 The story recounts the treachery of two judges who try to blackmail the beautiful Susanna into having sexual relations. Her fidelity to God and to her integrity strengthen her to refuse, even in the face of death. (Because of the length of the reading, it is suggested that six readers be used:
Reader 1 Daniel 13:1–18
Reader 2 Daniel 13:19–27
Reader 3 Daniel 13:28–41
Reader 4 Daniel 13:42–49
Reader 5 Daniel 13:50–59
Reader 6 Daniel 13:60–63)

Quiet Time
(A few minutes of silence with appropriate soft music)

Leader Susanna faced terrible pressure to conform to the wishes of the elders—she was like us—but she resisted. Her integrity, the value she placed on being true to herself and faithful to her God, was greater than the threats made by the elders. Susanna knew who she was. She knew her true value lies in affirming boldly who she was and what she valued. God was at work in her conscience.

We too are sometimes caught in situations where we are tempted to conform, to give in to the threats or the enticements of the crowd. Let us pray that we know our values, that we treasure our integrity, our conscience, that we find the courage to be our best selves when we are tempted to go along with the crowd and settle for less.

Response

Leader   (Invite all the teenagers to sit, with the exception of four people standing scattered throughout the congregation.) Who will dare to stand when all others are seated? Who will speak a word of prayer to God when so many voices have fallen silent?

Pray-er 1   (standing) I stand when all sit. I pray when other voices have fallen silent. Lord, it is hard to stand out from the crowd. It is hard to be myself and not give in to peer pressure. Help me to know myself. Help me to know you and pray to you when so many say you don't care. Help me to be myself at all times and under all circumstances. For this I humbly pray . . .

All   Amen. (One-quarter of those present stand.)

Pray-er 2   (standing) I, too, stand before my God. I pray for courage to choose what is right when many lead me to choose what is wrong. I thank God for my conscience and for my own set of values to guide me. For this I pray . . .

All   Amen. (Another quarter stand.)

Pray-er 3   (standing) I dare to stand and pray for those who are alone and overcome by peer pressure. May these people know they can always change and make new decisions. May they know the warmth of your friendship, God. May they know you always stand with them, no matter what. For this I pray . . .

All   Amen. (One-quarter stand.)

Pray-er 4   (standing) I pray to the God of Susanna, to the God Jesus named father, to the God who speaks to each of us through our conscience. Help us to listen to your voice within, loving God, more than we listen to voices that would lead us astray. Speak to us and give us ears that really listen and a heart that is true to ourselves and true to you.

All   Amen. (The rest of the participants stand.)

Leader   Sometimes we need to stand alone in order to be true to who we are. Sometimes others will stand with us. Always God will stand with us through our conscience, through the sacraments, and through people who care for us. For this we thank the Lord.

All   Amen.

7

Born to Compete
Winning and Fair Play

Preparing for Prayer

Times for Use
•before an athletic event
•before an exam
•confirmation preparation, on justice or fortitude
•in conjunction with athletic banquet
•feast of St. Paul

Materials Needed
•felt markers
•sheets of white paper
•chalkboard, or newsprint
•graphic in large letters WE'RE NUMBER ONE
•athletic equipment, such as balls, gloves, shoes, etc.

Introduction
Sports, amateur or professional, control vast amounts of time, resources, money, and psychic energy in our society. What begins as a childhood game often ends as a multi-million-dollar business. The competition that develops one's character and sharpens one's skills is later often governed by a mindset that views the opposing athlete or team as an obstacle to fame and money, that views winning as the only purpose of athletics. Learning fair play and teamwork can easily be sacrificed to winning at any cost. The goal of this prayer service is to extol the important role of athletics for teaching discipline and fair play and the ability to compete with oneself.

Shared Experience
Invite the participants to write as many phrases about competition and winning as they can remember. For example: Nice guys finish last;

No one remembers who finished second; Winning isn't the main thing—it's the only thing. Afterward, ask for their responses and write some of these on a chalkboard or newsprint. Ask what the message of these sayings is for them. Are sports, competition, and winning being overemphasized? Does this block the development of the skills needed for cooperation? Do winning and losing lead to thinking of people in general as winners and losers? Are the qualities of fair play, teamwork, and competing with oneself being learned or ignored?

Allow discussion of these questions. Point out the need for balance in order to become a whole person. Comment on the benefits of competing against oneself to achieve one's own personal best. Highlight the need in today's world for qualities that will help us to cooperate and work together in order to solve the common problems facing people everywhere. Finally, point to the need for economic justice, in race relations, and in sharing Earth's resources. Fair play is a good preparation for this.

Prayer Service

Focus Prayer

Leader

Lord, we live in a world where sports, competition, and winning are emphasized daily. It is hard not to think of winning and competition as necessary to our happiness. Help us to see, Lord, that unrestrained competition makes everyone our enemy, and winning at any cost destroys relationships and the cooperation necessary for a society that respects all people. We look to you for help in developing a healthy sense of fair play and justice and an ability to develop our best skills without thinking of others as losers. Amen.

All

Amen.

Through God's Eyes

Leader

I wonder how God views the abundance of athletic events we see each week at school and on TV. I wonder if God has an opinion about winning at all costs and looking at some people as losers. I wonder if God believes and wants me to believe that winning is the only thing. Ask yourselves these questions as you listen to this word from holy scripture.

Reading

Reader

St. Paul use athletic training and competition as a metaphor for the fortitude and discipline he brings to a life of spreading God's word. A reading from St. Paul's first letter to the Corinthians (9:24–27)

Quiet Time

(A few minutes of silence with appropriate soft music)

Leader

St. Paul uses athletics to describe how he disciplines himself to live the gospel. He encourages us to strive to win, that is, achieve the goal of our personal life to live as Christians. Athletics and winning have their place, but they are secondary to embracing Christ's invitation to love. Jesus said that we would be judged his followers if we love one another, not if we defeat one another. Paul speaks of disciplining his body so it obeys him, to have control of his instinctual drives in the battle against addictions and sinful habits that would separate him from God's love. What a wonderful model for us.

Reprinted with permission from 20 More Teen Prayer Services by Kevin Regan
© 1994 Twenty-Third Publications, P.O. Box 180, Mystic, CT 06355. 800-321-0411

Let us be involved in athletics and compete, but let's compete against ourselves and let's learn to be disciplined so that we can say no to the forces in our world that would destroy our freedom. Let's compete knowing that winning isn't everything. Fair play, learning to cooperate with others as we work toward a common goal, learning to develop our talents and to admit our mistakes, learning to take pride in our own accomplishments and in the accomplishments of others—these are the real lessons of athletic competition.

Response
(Divide the participants into two teams. It could be girls against the boys or people on the left versus people on the right. Have the opposing teams line up and turn their backs toward each other.)

Pray-er 1   We will now offer our prayers to God taking three different positions. God of power and God of strength, often our desire to develop our abilities, to grow strong physically and to identify with our team have left us isolated from one another and looking at those who cannot achieve as we do as losers. Free us from the need to win at all cost and from judging as losers those whose God-given ability is different from our own. Let us pray to our God.

Left Side   We pray for freedom, Lord.

Right Side   We pray for freedom, Lord.
(Sides turn and face each other.)

Pray-er 2   Look, Lord, at what our competing has done. We look at each other across a great divide we have created. Our competition has been against each other, instead of with ourselves. In taking pride in our own gifts, we have left out those less gifted and now we don't know how to work together. Teach us to compete with our own personal best. Help us to learn teamwork so we can tackle together the evils that threaten our world. Let us pray to our God.

Right Side   Teach us cooperation, Lord. Break down the walls that separate us.

Left Side   Teach us cooperation, Lord. Break down the walls that separate us.

(The two groups merge and each person holds the hand of someone from the other side.)

Pray-er 3   God of all games and sports, you have created us with great athletic ability. Teach us to develop our gifts to the fullest. As one voice let us pray to the Lord.

All   Help us to develop all the talents you have given us, Lord.

Pray-er 4   Teach us not to use our gifts as a way to dominate others or to feel superior toward them; instead, help us to use our gifts to build bridges of understanding and compassion between one another. As one voice, let us pray to the Lord.

All   Help us, Lord, to love and be compassionate.

Pray-er 5   We have joined hands as a sign of our unity. Guide us to a way of life that is fair and just for all. And may all of our competing and striving lead to you and your unconditional love. As one voice, let us pray to the Lord.

All   Lord, in all our effort and striving, you be great in us. Amen, Amen.

8

The Cross of Courage
Doing What Is Right

Preparing for Prayer

Times for Use
• retreat day dealing with values
• confirmation preparation, on courage or decision making
• class dealing with alcohol, peer pressure, or sexual behavior
• feast of the Holy Cross

Materials Needed
• newsprint on a stand

Introduction
Struggle, taking up the cross of Jesus, is a necessary part of the Christian life. The disciple, although rooted in Christ by baptism, lives in a sinful world that he and she must constantly struggle against. This takes courage. The tension of living as a Christian in a sinful world can be creative, leading to growth, or it can be threatening, leading people to give up the struggle. Our young people know how difficult the Christian way of life can be in a world of easy alcohol, drugs, and sex. The gospel invites them to grow in love, to become genuine Christian witnesses. This service recognizes the place of the cross in this transforming process.

Shared Experience
Begin by mentioning how hard it is to do what is right, perhaps with an example from your own experience. At times, we all find it more convenient to take the easy way out, to give in to peer pressure, to go back on our word. Invite the participants to think of a time they failed to do what was right and to name what led them to give in to evil rather than choose the good. Help them with examples: Was it peer pressure, the desire

to fit in with the group, lack of concern, the desire to feel good or have a good time? Write a sampling of their responses on the newsprint. Next, ask them what they need in order to do what is right. Courage? Guidance? Some may need the ability to say no to their appetites or to develop a better self-image.

Prayer Service

Focus Prayer

Leader   God, it is sometimes a heavy cross for us to carry doing what we know is right, saying no to what we would would like to do. Give us the courage to be true to our best selves and to be true to our calling to follow you.

All   Amen. We pray in the name of your son.

Through God's Eyes

Leader   To be at a party and not to take a drink, to be pressured into sexual behavior and to be able to say I'm not ready, to refuse to join the group making fun of a classmate, to be pregnant, alone, and frightened and not seek an abortion: It takes courage to do the right thing and to say no to what is easy, or popular. Let's listen to a passage from scripture where Jesus reminds us it will be a cross to say no to ourselves in order to follow his values, his way of living.

Reading

Reader 1   We now listen to Jesus' challenge that if his disciples today really want to love and follow him, they better be prepared to pay a price. A reading from the holy gospel according to Matthew (16:24–28)

Quiet Time

(A few minutes of silence with appropriate soft music.)

Leader   Perhaps you know the story of the boy who couldn't say no. He was very bright and had a winning personality but he was very self-centered and couldn't say no to himself. As a child, he always had to get his own way, and he lost friends because of this. As a teenager, he wanted to play high school basketball but was too lazy to work out or go to practice. He wanted to do well in school, but found it easier to spend hours watching television. He wanted to be in control of his life but his inability to say no to himself made him an easy mark for the drug dealer. It wasn't until he found himself arrested for buying a controlled substance that he sought help and began to turn his life around.

    Jesus asks us to carry our cross, to say no to our selfish urges in order to be able to grow and mature into people in control of

Reprinted with permission from *20 More Teen Prayer Services* by Kevin Regan
© 1994 Twenty-Third Publications, P.O. Box 180, Mystic, CT 06355. 800-321-0411

their lives, people able to give themselves to the difficult challenges that love places before them. Join me in prayer that we may see the cross not as an obstacle, but as a way to freedom and a way to living passionately like Jesus.

Response

Leader   All of us want to be free but have difficulty saying no to those forces that block our freedom to love and do the right thing. Join me in prayer that we may encourage one another to choose to carry the cross of following Jesus.

Pray-er 1   When it is difficult, Jesus, to say no to alcohol or drugs, help us to carry our cross and say yes to freedom. We pray . . .

All   We say yes, Lord.

Pray-er 2   When we are lazy, squandering our talents, help us to carry our cross and say yes to work and perseverance. We pray . . .

All   We say yes, Lord.

Pray-er 3   When we are not ready, Lord, to take responsibility for the consequences of a sexual encounter, help us to be true to ourselves and carry the cross of saying no so that we may say yes to what is best in ourselves. We pray . . .

All   We say yes, Lord.

Pray-er 4   Jesus, when we are in trouble and all seems lost, help us to find a friend, someone who will be there for us and let them help us to carry our cross. We pray . . .

All   We say yes, Lord.

Leader   May God give each of you the courage to choose to do what is right. May you find in Jesus a true friend to whom you can give your complete trust. And may God help you to do what is right and bless you. Amen.

9

People to Imitate
Heroes

Preparing for Prayer

Times for Use
• career day
• when athlete, singer, or movie star role models are in the news
• confirmation preparation, on the saints
• All Saints Day

Materials Needed
• pictures of celebrities from movies, TV, music, and athletics
• pictures of canonized saints and saintly average folks, along with pictures of the teenagers present at the service, placed around the assembly place
• table in front of the assembly
• 4 lecterns

Introduction
Who are the models worthy of imitation by the youth of today? Lucky the student enticed into the adventure of learning by a gifted teacher, the daughter or son whose best role model is their mother or father, the athlete who learns from his coach to develop athletic skills, along with the qualities needed for being human. Role models are essential to motivate, direct, and challenge the young to imagine and develop what is best within themselves. A false individualism common in our society says there is no need for models; we'll each "do our own thing." This service calls attention to the lives and qualities of people who model courageous Christian living for the young. Such people can satisfy the thirst of teenagers for genuine heroes who can excite and ignite them to dream of a more human world and to work courageously and compassionately to make that world a reality.

Shared Experience

Leader Look at the pictures scattered around the room and ask yourself if any of these people could be a hero for you. You may think you have no heroes, that there is no need for models for you to imitate or be inspired by. But I ask you to think carefully and ask yourselves: Don't we all need people to look up to? Don't we all need people who will awaken us to what is best in us, inspire us, and challenge us to do better? Don't we need those who by their lives inspire us to dream and to work harder to be our best and to build a better, more human world? Perhaps the following will help us to think about heroes.

(Four lecterns may be placed in front of the assembly. The leader may wish to prepare four biographies of traditional saints.)

Narrator Who can name someone who is a role model for you?

Speaker 1 I don't pick anyone famous, but rather I choose my mother. She has had it tough since my father died but she never complains. She works hard each day to provide for my sister, my brother, and myself. But she always finds time to listen to our problems and offer advice when we seek it. She finds time to help out at church and goes to as many of our games as she can. She has taught me not to complain or to pity myself, but to be generous and to see how I can be there for others. When I reach out to other people, I sometimes see the world through her eyes, and this gives me a different view of my own problems. She is really my best friend.

Speaker 2 I like to think of myself as pretty independent, but there are people who get me to think about where I am going in life. I get goosebumps whenever I listen to Dr. King's "I have a dream" speech, when I think of his love for his people that led him to stay involved when things got really rough, and his willingness to challenge injustice with nonviolent action. These are qualities I hope to make my own. That is a real challenge to me.

Speaker 3 I remember the words of Maryknoll Sister Ita Ford. She was an American nun murdered by the military of El Salvador. She spoke out about the unjust way the peasants were being treated and she worked hard among them to make things better. Shortly before she died, she wrote in a letter that we shouldn't waste our gifts and the opportunities we have to make ourselves and others happy. She is my model. I want to use every opportunity I have to help others and bring contentment into the world.

Narrator   I hope these examples are enough to help you to think of the models in your life. Who are the people who you can look up to and who challenge you to get beyond mediocrity to develop what is best in you?

Leader   Take a moment to write the name(s) of people who are a model for the kind of person you want to become. After you have written one or two names, share them with the person next to you and explain why you chose this person. Hold on to your papers.

Prayer Service

Focus Prayer

Leader   Let us focus on our need for heroes and thank God for the heroes who walk among us each day. For those in our families who give us wonderful examples of how to live. For those who teach and coach and guide us into becoming our best selves. For those in political life, religious life, economic life, and in the world of athletics and entertainment who give us wonderful examples of the Christian life, let us pray to the Lord . . .

All   God, we thank you for giving us models to follow.

Through God's Eyes

Leader   Do you agree we all need people to inspire us? Do you believe as I do that it is critical that we have genuine heroes to guide us to develop what is best in ourselves? Like a lighthouse that guides ships through turbulent waters, role models offer direction and guidance to our personal ships trying to navigate through the high seas and hurricanes of life. Scripture is a storehouse of heroes worthy of our study and imitation. Ruth and Deborah, Jonathan and David, Susanna and Samson are a few. In the following passages we meet some of the less noticed heroes designated such by Jesus. (Any one or all of the following readings may be used.)

Reading

Reader 1   In the account of the centurion's servant, Jesus holds up the faith of the centurion as a worthy model for all to follow. A reading from the holy gospel according to St. Luke (7:1–10)

Reader 2   In the account of the widow's mite, Jesus extols the generosity of the widow as a model worthy of our imitation. A reading from the gospel according to St. Mark (12:42–44)

Reader 3   Jesus shows his followers that there is real greatness in being unassuming and childlike. A reading from the holy gospel according to St. Luke (9:46–48)

Quiet Time

(A few minutes of silence with appropriate soft music)

Leader   You notice that Jesus didn't pick extraordinary people who could be heroes for us. He picked a Roman centurion, a child, a poor widow. It wasn't their titles or their power or wealth that made these people worthy of recognition for Jesus. It was the quality of their character, the depth of their soul. Jesus knew generosity wasn't about how much a person gave but how much a person had left over after giving. He realized that faith wasn't about whether we get what we pray for, but rather about abandonment and trust in another person. And Jesus knew greatness is not about having power or wealth but about humility and awe and the wonder of children. All of Jesus' heroes are notable because they are so simple, so ordinary. They are worthy of attention because each has discovered what is really important in life, what is really lasting: faith, love, and God's will.

Response

Leader   As a way of responding with gratitude for the models God has given us, we will come forward one at a time and place the paper with the name of our hero on the table. Say the name aloud and anything you want to add. The rest of us will respond: For men and women of courage and faith, we thank you, Lord.

(The following are given as examples. You may want to select a few young people beforehand to present their names or to create a list of heroes as representative of the community. A list with some of the traditional saints and their accomplishments can also be used.)

Speaker 1   For my mother and father who are unselfish in their love for me . . .

All   For men and women of courage and faith, we thank you, Lord.

Speaker 2   For Dr. Martin Luther King, Jr. who fought courageously to free the oppressed . . .

All   For women and men of courage and faith, we thank you, Lord.

Speaker 3   For Dorothy Day who cared for the poor and promoted the gospel call to nonviolence . . .

All   For men and women of courage and faith, we thank you, Lord.

Speaker 4   For the six Jesuit priests, their housekeeper and her daughter, who were martyred supporting the poor in El Salvador. . .

All	For women and men of courage and faith, we thank you, Lord.
Speaker 5	For those we know who are courageously dealing with sickness and disease . . .
All	For men and women of courage and faith, we thank you, Lord.
Leader	God, you bless us in every age with women and men who can inspire us to do great things for you. Help us to find role models who exemplify what is the best in being human and being a disciple of your son. Teach us to be thankful for those who live so passionately and justly that they are a light for us on our way to you. We pray in the name of Jesus.
All	Amen.

10

Growing Together
Life in the Family

Preparing for Prayer

Times for Use
• family retreat
• family picnic
• prayer service for families
• confirmation preparation, on the gift of family
• feast of the Holy Family
• Mother's Day
• Father's Day
• feast of St. Joseph

Materials Needed
• pictures of Jesus, Mary, and Joseph
• pictures of families involved in various activites
• drawing paper
• markers, pens, or pencils

Introduction
As Christians, we believe in a God who is a family, the Blessed Trinity. Our familes, when united in love, image the union of Father, Son, and Holy Spirit. They also mirror to all the world Christ's living covenant with the church.

In this service it is important to remember that many types of families exist in our parishes today. The teenagers in the assembly will not all be from the traditional family unit, as we have thought of it (mother and father in their first marriage with their biological children). This is no longer the predominant family unit in the parish, not nearly. There are single-parent (never married, or divorced, or widowed) families; interracial families; families with remarried parents; familes with adopted children; families even with same-sex parents. This service celebrates the gift of a loving family, no matter what form it may take in the concrete.

Shared Experience

Invite the participants to look at the pictures of families you have gathered and ask them to think for a moment about their own family. Ask them what comes to mind when they think of family. Place some of these responses on newsprint. Next, ask them to write on a piece of paper two things they value that they learned from their families and two things that sometimes make living in a family difficult. These should be done quietly by themselves and then the paper folded in half.

Prayer Service

Focus Prayer

Leader
Families give us life. Most of the important things we know we have learned from our families. We pray for loving families. You nurture us like a loving mother and protect us like a caring father. Help all mothers and fathers to be understanding and patient and role models we can imitate. Help us to be forgiving of failures and readily involved in our family life so that they may reflect your love for us. For this we pray to you, Jesus, our brother and friend.

All
Amen.

Through God's Eyes

Leader
In our families we experience love and joy, as well as confusion and tension. There are no perfect families. This is why forgiveness is so important. It mends the hurt we inflict unintentionally on one another. Some families may have special problems, such as alcoholism. In other families there may even be physical and sexual abuse. People who abuse others need the help of specially trained people before they can live productively in a family. But families are also a place of love, respect, and discipline. This is the atmosphere we need to develop as mature, loving people. This we celebrate in prayer.

Reading

Reader
Like us, Jesus experienced the ups and downs of family life. Let us listen together to one account of life in his family. A reading from the holy gospel according to St. Luke (2:41–52)

Quiet Time
(A few minutes of silence with appropriate soft music)

Leader
In this passage, we see a young Jesus so enthusiastic about what he is doing that he forgets to tell his parents where he is. How much like us when it comes to curfew and friends. But Jesus went obediently with Mary and Joseph because he knew they would support the values of truthfulness, honesty, love of neighbor and of God that would be so important for his work as an adult. He learned from his family how to laugh and play and work and stand up for the poor. If we can, let us thank

Reprinted with permission from *20 More Teen Prayer Services* by Kevin Regan
© 1994 Twenty-Third Publications, P.O. Box 180, Mystic, CT 06355. 800-321-0411

God for our families. If we can't because of hurt, let us at least pray for them and that we may be loving parents and husbands and wives when we have families of our own.

Response
(The participants are invited to hold hands or to link arms as a sign of being part of the larger family of the church.)

Leader   Our God is a family God of three persons in the unity of love. We are made in God's image through our family life and through being responsible members of the human family. Let us pray as we hear different types of families described.

Speaker 1   When I hear the word family, I think of a mother and father and children living together. They share experiences together, learn how to give and receive affection, how to resolve conflict, and learn what values are important in life. Pray with me in thanksgiving for the love, support, and guidance traditional families provide. Let us pray . . .

All   Holy Trinity, family God, we thank you for the love of our families.

Speaker 2   When I hear the word "family," I think of my mom. My father left us, my little brother, my mom, and me, four years ago. He just walked out. My mom decided to stand by us. She has worked hard to create a loving home for me and my brother. Family is not just something we are born into, but it is something created by those who choose to stick by us and love us through hard times. Let us pray . . .

All   Holy Trinity, family God, we thank you for the love of our families.

Speaker 3   I lived in a foster home for four years before I was adopted. At first I was really tough on my adoptive parents. I was so afraid they did not really love me that I wanted them to prove their love. I have learned about anger and sorrow and loneliness, but also from my adoptive parents about acceptance and sharing and joy. They have taught me that I have to discover who I am and how I want to live my life. No one can tell me that. Let us pray . . .

All	Holy Trinity, family God, we thank you for the love of our families.
Speaker 4	Some day some of us will be married and have a family of our own. Help us to prepare now to be loving, forgiving, and unselfish so that we may create loving families that are pleasing to God. Let us pray . . .
All	Holy Trinity, family God, we thank you for the love of our families.
Leader	Jesus, in your family you learned to love God and love those around you, especially the poor and the forgotten. Teach us to be grateful for the good our families have shared with us and to be forgiving for the ways our families have failed us. Help us to go out from our families to create one family in our world where each person is treated with respect and dignity, let us pray . . .
All	Holy Trinity, family God, we thank you for your love and for the love of our families. Amen.

(If the shared experience was completed, you may invite the young people to share their papers with one another to learn how others experience family.) |

11

Called to Be Witnesses
The Joy of Being Disciple

Preparing for Prayer

Times for Use
• vocation or career day
• confirmation preparation, on discipleship
• Pentecost
• Christ the King

Materials Needed
• pictures of current world events
• camera
• bread dough
• newsprint sheets

Introduction
We are all called to revel in the way we live the values inherent in what we teach or believe. That is, we and our adolescents are called as Christians to witness to the values, the mindset of Jesus. The presence of God's Spirit in the lives of Jesus' first disciples made them witnesses. The presence of the Spirit in our lives also calls us to be witnesses. This is what we celebrate in this prayer service.

Shared Experience
Explain that we are going to show the difference between admiring a set of values or way of life, and actually mirroring these values in the way one lives. If possible, have enough bread dough for each person or groups of two to knead the dough. All others who have brought cameras are to take pictures and then to join in the kneading. (A Polaroid camera would allow for immediate viewing.) Allow the teenagers to form the dough into

any shape they want as long as it will fit into a baking pan. When the dough is ready, have it put aside for baking. Allow time for the participants to clean their hands.

Ask them the difference between taking a picture of people making bread and actually making the bread. These responses may be listed on newsprint. Help them to reflect on the participation needed to make the bread. Some of them didn't just record what happened as a camera does; they were involved in kneading the dough, forming it, and determining the quality of the bread-making. Point out that as Christians they are witnesses to Jesus, his values, and his work to establish God's reign on Earth. They are invited not only to listen to the words of the gospel passively, like a camera taking pictures, but to be "doers," witnesses to God's love by living the values Jesus lived. God's Holy Spirit is within them to help them live as witnesses in today's world.

Prayer Service

Focus Prayer

Leader   We pray that we may understand what it means to be witnesses to the life and values of Jesus in today's world. Help us to read the gospel as your word addressed to us personally, showing us the way to happiness and life.

All   Amen.

Through God's Eyes

Leader   If you have seen a car accident, you have felt the need to tell others exactly what happened. If you have experienced the joy of a wedding, you have told your friends what the bride wore, who were in the wedding party, and what the reception was like. If you experienced a thrilling ballgame, you have told others they should have been there. When we witness something exciting or meaningful, we share it with others. It was because the words and works of Jesus were so revolutionary that they changed the lives of the first disciples and made them want to spread his word throughout the world. We too are called by God to know Jesus and grow in faith so that his words and actions may penetrate our hearts and we may experience the transforming power of his life. Then we are ready to be witnesses of his words and works because we know they are revolutionary and offer life and hope to our world. We will listen to the call of the first witnesses.

Reading

Reader   The gospel tells the story of the miraculous catch of fish and the call of the first disciples. A reading from the holy gospel according to St. Luke (5:1–11)

Quiet Time

(A few minutes of silence with appropriate soft music)

Leader   You all know what it's like to be called to do a specific task. Some of you play sports and know how great it feels when the coach sends you in with a play. Some of you know how great it feels to be called to act in a school play. Others know the feeling of being named class president or head of a club. Another type of call is the one God makes, that we may be witnesses to the life and love of Jesus. We need not only to know *about*

Reprinted with permission from *20 More Teen Prayer Services* by Kevin Regan
© 1994 Twenty-Third Publications, P.O. Box 180, Mystic, CT 06355. 800-321-0411

Jesus, but to know Jesus personally, intimately. Reading scripture, praying, attending liturgy, and becoming involved in retreats are excellent ways to do this. Ultimately we are called to let Jesus' love transform our lives. I hope that this may happen for you. Let us pray now for one another that we may know Jesus and be his witnesses to help transform the world.

Response

Leader   Let us pray together that we may be Jesus' witnesses in the world. (You will need three pray-ers and someone to represent Jesus.)

Reader 1   This is an age of violence. Fighting, to some, is the only way to solve conflicts. Firearms are the second leading cause of death for people 15-19 years of age. Let us listen to the words of Jesus.

Jesus   You are blessed when you are peacemakers. If you are my witnesses, you try to overcome evil and violence with goodness and love. Now pray to God who loves you . . .

All   Teach us peace in a violent world. Teach us to be your witnesses, Lord.

Reader 2   This is an age of casual sex. There are over one million teenage pregnancies each year in the United States. Too often people end relationships by hurting themselves and each other. Relationships end in pain, anger, and a feeling of rejection. Let us listen to the words of Jesus.

Jesus   If you are my witnesses, you will love one another. Love is patient, love is kind. Love never uses another person or rejoices over evil. Love bears all things and endures all things. If you are my witnesses, you will wait until you are ready for the permanent commitment necessary for sexual union to express love. Now pray to God who loves you . . .

All   Teach us to wait until we are ready for the responsibility of a permanent commitment which sexual union implies. Teach us to be your witnesses, Lord.

Reader 3   This is an age of greed and consumption. Success is measured by the size of my bank account, and happiness is in proportion to the number and size of the things I own. Let us listen to the words of Jesus.

Jesus   You can not serve God and money, for you will hate one and serve the other. Because I am with you and you are my friends, serving those in greatest need and healing those in pain will make you truly great and bring you unimagined joy. Now pray to God who loves you.

All   Teach us to overcome slavery to money through service to one another. Teach us to be your witnesses, Lord. (If the Shared Experience activity was completed, the participants will be invited to bless the bread. Raising their hands over the bread, they say: "Blessed are you, Lord God of all creation, from your goodness we have this bread to offer. Accept it and our lives as our gift to you. May the strength we gain from eating it help us to become your disciples. Amen.")

         (If the Shared Experience was not used, add the following.)
Leader   God, we thank you for the gift of your son, Jesus. May we discover the joy of being his witnesses in our homes, at school, on the playing field, and wherever we may be.

All   Amen.

12

Dare to Dream
Vocation

Preparing for Prayer

Times for Use
• career days
• vocation retreats
• day of recollection
• service projects for confirmation preparation
• Pentecost
• feast of the Baptism of the Lord

Materials Needed
• 4 Christians to talk briefly about their vocations

Introduction
What do teenagers base their career choices on? Money? Job security? Chance? Christian humanism challenges them to look at their lives as a call from God to use their gifts to better the human community and to play a real part in establishing God's reign on Earth. Jesus' invitation to follow him is a call to transform the world "in Christ." It is the purpose of this prayer service to call attention to this call and to help the teenagers to allow it to become part of their lives.

Shared Experience
Leader   Each of us will someday choose a career or a job that we hope will bring us happiness. But how do we choose what we will do and how do we know whether it will make us happy? We have invited four speakers who have found meaning and purpose in what they do. Listen to what they have to say, and then you will have the opportunity to ask questions. (The first speaker is introduced. After introducing the other speakers, allow time for questions and offer thanks to the speakers.)

Prayer Service

Focus Prayer

Leader   Loving God, you have created us with different talents and you have placed people in our world who need the specific gift that each of us can offer. Help us to think about our future life as a way to answer your call to develop and use our gifts for the good of the community. Grant us the courage and wisdom to respond generously to your call. We pray this with faith in your love for us.

All   Amen.

Through God's Eyes

Leader   We have many guides to help us think about the future. Some tell us our futures are ways to make money and accumulate material goods. Others tell us that career advancement and power are all that matter. But there are other, more penetrating voices who see that our futures are intimately bound to God's presence in the world. These people encourage us to realize that our ability to solve problems, imagine new futures, design or repair machines, care for and educate children, cure diseases, are ways that God calls us to continue to bring Christ's love into the world. As we think about our futures, let us listen to God's word and allow its message to penetrate our hearts.

Reading

Reader   This reading describes Samuel's failure to recognize that God was calling him, until Eli told him it was the Lord. A reading from the first book of Samuel (3:1–9)

Quiet Time

(A few minutes of silence with appropriate soft music)

Leader   This reading is a reminder that as followers of Jesus, baptized in his name, God calls us to use our gifts for the service of our sisters and brothers. When we realize that we have a special talent, do we think of it as God's way of calling us to a particular vocation in life? For Mother Teresa it was the sight of an abandoned child that helped her to discover her vocation. For my nephew, it was hearing a speaker at college. For the monk and writer, Thomas Merton, it was his best friend and his

Reprinted with permission from *20 More Teen Prayer Services* by Kevin Regan
© 1994 Twenty-Third Publications, P.O. Box 180, Mystic, CT 06355. 800-321-0411

teachers in college who helped him to discover his vocation in life. Whatever our talents, God invites us to use them for more than making money, gaining security, or finding "success." For we are called by God to heal the brokenness of the world.

Think for a moment of Mother Teresa who encourages us to give of ourselves until it hurts. Or Dr. Albert Schweitzer who cautioned us that only those who learn how to serve will be really happy. Are you familiar with the beautiful thoughts of Sr. Ita Ford, martyred in El Salvador? She tried to help her niece Jennifer think about the future. She wrote to her: "What I'm saying is I hope you find what gives life a deep meaning for you. Something worth living or maybe even worth dying for—something that energizes you, enthuses you and enables you to keep moving ahead." This I believe is what God wants for each of you.

Response

Leader	Let us pray to the Holy Spirit who is our protector and guides us in all our decisions.
Pray-er 1	Spirit of truth, Sr. Ita Ford invites us to find what will give deep meaning to our lives. Help us to seek what is meaningful for us. (Invite all to pause to consider what may give meaning to their lives.) For the gift of knowing what will bring us meaning, let us pray to the Spirit of truth . . .
All	Holy Spirit, help us to find meaning, help us to find truth.
Pray-er 2	Spirit of life, Sr. Ita Ford invites us to find something worth living for, something worth dying for. Help us to discover something so precious that it is worthy of our talents, even the gift of our lives. (Have the participants think for a moment about a career that is worthy of their gifts.) For the gift of knowing what is worthy of our gifts, what is worthy of our lives, let us pray to the Spirit of life . . .
All	Holy Spirit, help us to find meaning, help us to find truth.
Pray-er 3	Spirit of the future, Sr. Ita Ford invites us to find what will energize and enthuse us and keep us going. (Have the participants ask God to help them know what life's work will energize them and keep them going when times are difficult.) In a world where work has become only a task, a boring ne-

cessity for so many, help us, Holy Spirit, to face the future with great hope, confident that God calls us not to a job but to a way of life in Christ's love. Let us pray to the God of the future . . .

All   Holy Spirit, help us to find meaning, help us to find truth.

Leader   We have in faith asked God's help in deciding our futures. Let us show that we trust God and have confidence in God's presence by offering to one another a sign of peace.

13

One With Earth
Loving the Planet that Sustains Us

Preparing for Prayer

Times for Use
•Earth Day
•field trip, such as a whale watch
•confirmation preparation, on environment, co-creation
•Arbor Day
•feast of St. Francis

Materials Needed
•newsprint sheets
•felt-tip marker
•bowl of water
•dish of soil
•small plant
•fruit or vegetable
•sweater
•candle
•container with a flower seed in soil for each participant

Introduction
The warning signs are everywhere present. A 1992 report of the National Academy of Sciences and the Royal Society of London tells us that if predictions of population growth hold true with unchanged patterns of human activity, neither science or technology can prevent further degradation of the environment and continued poverty for much of the world. The Sierra Club reminds us that we in the U.S. dump 2.7 billion pounds of toxins into the air every year, discharge 500 million pounds of toxic waste into our rivers, and bury 160 million tons of trash. The work for justice and

peace in our world, the desire for the spiritual transformation of unjust structures are intimately bound to a right relationship to the environment. Native American George Tinker reminds us that the call of Jesus to repentance and establishing God's reign is a call to be in right relationship to creation and the Creator. This prayer service is to help the teenagers realize that they are not *apart from* Earth but *a part of* it, and to recognize the urgency of the work at hand and to celebrate the interdependence of all creatures loved and redeemed by Christ.

Shared Experience

Invite the participants to look at the plant and other gifts from the environment you have assembled. Ask them to name some of the many gifts Earth provides. Write these on the newsprint. Next, ask them to name the threats to the environment that they are familiar with. Help them to make connections between their lifestyles and the environment. Remind them that they are a part of creation and that God requires us to use the environment as a trust, to protect it and use it responsibly, to care for it so that all may share equally in its abundance, and it may flourish for future generations. (You may want to use as a resource the Environmental Almanac compiled by the World Resources Institute.)

Prayer Service

Focus Prayer

Leader   God, creator of all living and non-living beings, you have made us a part of this universe with the great responsibility to learn about it, love it, and use it wisely with moderation. Your son's resurrection frees us from sin and death and gives us hope that all creation will share in his glory forever. Let us pray that we faithfully carry out our role in this great drama.

All   Amen.

Through God's Eyes

Leader   Perhaps we sometimes take for granted the many gifts our environment provides for us. Not only food, drink, shelter, and clothing, but materials for work, raw materials for the artist and musician to create works of beauty. The environment provides refreshment in the summer and recreation in the winter. It is through the environment that we experience wonder and awe and learn we are part of a much larger whole. Jesus took the ordinary gifts of nature—bread, wine, oil—and gave these the power to unite us with himself. He invites us today to carry on the work of God's love by learning to love Mother Earth and to use it in such a way that its treasures are preserved for future generations, and its abundance is justly available to all people. One of the greatest images of peace is one offered by the prophet Isaiah who sees in the peaceable kingdom all the contrary forces of creation in harmony and peace with one another. Let's listen to one reading from the Hebrew scriptures and one from the Christian scriptures that speak of the spiritual meaning of right relationship to the environment.

Reading

Reader 1   Isaiah descibes the messianic age as one full of peace and justice flowing from the knowledge of the Lord. A reading from the book of the prophet Isaiah (11:6–9)

Reader 2   In this reading St. Paul sees all creation as flowing from and back to Christ. It is in Christ that all unity exists, and through the resurrection that all creation will be reconciled in Christ. A reading from the letter to the Colossians (1:15–20)

Reprinted with permission from *20 More Teen Prayer Services* by Kevin Regan
© 1994 Twenty-Third Publications, P.O. Box 180, Mystic, CT 06355. 800-321-0411

Quiet Time
(A few minutes of silence with appropriate soft music)

Leader   What a spectacular view of creation Isaiah provides. He sees all creation moving toward a place of harmony and peace where no harm is done, where all creation shares in the unity of justice and peace. How can this be? St. Paul explains that all creation is finally unified and finds its fullest meaning in the death and resurrection of Christ. We are active members of Christ today and of creation itself; our role is to help every part of our environment to share in God's love. Love is to guide our relationship not only with other people, but with the environment for future generations. What a great adventure is ours!

Response
(If possible, those present should be standing around the symbols of the environment assembled.)

Leader   Let us pray to God that we may care for the gifts of creation and join ourselves to Christ's work of establishing God's reign through the reconciliation of all creatures.

Pray-er 1   (holding high the basin of water) You created the gift of water to nourish us, refresh us, and cleanse us. In baptism, water is the sign of our life as your children and members of your family. Help us, Creator God, to use water moderately. Help us never to waste it or take it for granted. We thank you for its awesome power, its spectacular beauty, its refreshing coolness.

Right Side   For water that fills Earth, joining continents and making deserts fertile, we thank you, loving creator. We pray for a just relationship to water and to all who depend upon water for life. For the gift of water we thank you, creator God.

Pray-er 2   (holding up the dish of soil) We thank you for the soil under our feet. We praise you for the fruit it provides. Help us to walk on Planet Earth with gratitude and with the intention to care for it.

Left Side   For the gift of soil and for the food it gives us, we thank you, God. Help us to realize that many different people walk this same planet and have a right to its resources. For the gift of Earth we thank you, creator God.

Pray-er 3	(holding the plant) We thank you for the plants, flowers, trees, and animals. They share with us the sun and water and soil and look to us for protection. You have taken the fruit of the wheat plant and used its bread as the means by which Jesus comes to nourish us with his life. Help us always to respect the plants and animals that journey with us on our way.
Right Side	Plants of every variety fill the planet, along with animals of every shape and size. Birds and reptiles too. We praise you, creator God for creating with so much variety. You dazzle us with the splendor of your gifts, the recklessness of your love. Help us to love all your creatures. For the gift of plants and animals we thank you, creator God.
Pray-er 4	(carefully raising the candle) This light is the fire of your creation, God, your life in us. At baptism we received a candle as a sign of your life burning in us. May we know the fire present in all creation. Help us to be on fire with a zeal for justice and a commitment to treat every gift of creation with respect and care.
Left Side	We praise you, giving God, for the gift of fire and for the fire of your love. Help us to be on fire with your vision, which takes us beyond sin and death. Give us the fire of truth so we will want to do your will. And may you always be the flame that burns within us. For the gift of fire we thank you, creator God.
Leader	Let us join hands as a sign that all things are connected and we have a responsibility to care for all. Let us raise our hands slowly as sign that all we do to God's creation we do to Christ. Let us now place our arms on each others' shoulders as a sign that we are one in God's Spirit and that we are called to bring healing to all God has created.

Come forward now for a seed to take home with you and plant. May you care for it and watch it grow. May it be a reminder that all creatures on Earth need care. God calls you to protect the environment so that all may share in its abundance. |
| All | Amen. Amen.
(Participants come forward to receive their seeds.) |

14

The Call to Forgive
Jesus' Way of Healing

Preparing for Prayer

Times for Use
• reconciliation service
• confirmation preparation, on forgiveness
• retreat, on healing relationships
• All Saints Day

Materials Needed
• broken piece of pottery
• picture of a potter or potter's wheel
• 3 stands

Introduction
If there is one characteristic of the follower of Christ, it is forgiveness. Over and over, in word and action, Jesus illustrated the absolute need both to seek forgiveness and to offer it to others. It is only through the forgiveness of our sins that we enter the new life of love that joins us to God. It is only through the forgiveness we offer that others may know God's love; through it the rift in human relationships is mended and the life of friendship renewed. This power of forgiveness to keep alive and renew human relationships, and to allow us to enter into God's own life, is what we celebrate.

Shared Experience
Place the two pieces of pottery on stands to the right and left of the picture of the potter or potter's wheel. Invite those present to look quietly for a moment at the piece of whole pottery, the picture of the potter, and the piece of broken pottery. Ask them to pick a partner, a friend if possible,

and invite them to sit facing each other. As they sit ask them to think of some of the things that make friendship so special. After a short time ask them to take their chairs and turn them back to back. Ask them to remember times friends have hurt them; invite them to feel the feelings they experienced then. You may offer some ideas to help with each reflection.

After the participants have shared their thoughts or feelings from the experience, explain that relationships are like a piece of pottery: meant to be whole but easily broken. Only through seeking forgiveness and offering forgiveness can relationships be mended. Forgiveness is the potter's hand molding, mending, making whole. One who can't forgive can't hope to have lasting and fulfilling relationships.

Prayer Service

Focus Prayer

Leader   All of us need to love and need others to love us. But we sometimes hurt one another. We break our bonds with our friends and therefore with God. Who can save us from the repeated pain caused by broken relationships? Will you save us, Lord?

All   Yes, Lord, we seek your pardon, we seek your peace.

Through God's Eyes

Leader   What is as painful as the betrayal by a friend? What is as lonely as being without your friend? It is certain is that friendships will be broken, and unless we want to walk through life alone we need to be able to ask for forgiveness and to extend forgiveness to those who seek it. If pride or stubbornness prevents us from bringing the healing power of forgiveness into our relationships, how can our relationships last? Our model of forgiveness is Jesus who entered into our world sinless, but made it clear that God is a forgiving God. Let us listen together to God's word of forgiveness.

Reading

(You may want to break the reading into four parts: the narrator, the younger son, the older son, and the father.)

Reader 1   This parable describes God's longing to forgive those who like the younger son choose what is destructive of themselves and their relationship to God. A reading from the holy gospel according to St. Luke (15:11–32)

Quiet Time

(A few minutes of silence with appropriate soft music)

Response

(If the sacrament of reconciliation is to be celebrated, it should be done at this time and the leader should close with the final prayer, on page 74. If confessions are not heard at this time, continue as follows.)

(The leader stands in the center, facing the assembly. The prayers should be sitting in 4 chairs with their backs to the assembly.)

Leader   We join now in prayer, seeking God's forgiveness for our sins.

Let us now pray for the courage to ask for forgiveness from those we harm and to extend forgiveness to those who seek it from us. *(pause)*

Pray-er 1   (stands and faces the assembly) Jesus, in the story of the Prodigal Son, you show us the joy with which you receive us back when we have sinned. We seek to repent of our sins. We seek your friendship. We seek your joy. And we pray . . .

Right Side   We seek your friendship, Lord. We seek your joy.

Leader   Through our failure to forgive each other, we carry grudges in our hearts where love belongs. We seek to turn back to you, Lord.

Pray-er 2   (facing the assembly) Lord, you seek to replace our hearts of stone with hearts of loving forgiveness. Help us to let go of grudges that destroy others and ourselves. We seek to learn your forgiveness. We seek to experience your joy. We pray . . .

Left Side   We seek your forgiveness, Lord. We seek your joy.

Leader   We sometimes hurt each other through a thoughtless comment or a harsh word. We turn our backs on each other. We turn our backs on you.

Pray-er 3   (facing the assembly) God of love, you remind us that the tongue can cut as sharply as a sword. Forgive us for the words we have spoken that have harmed our relationships with each other and with you. We seek your forgiveness, Lord. We seek your joy. We pray . . .

Right Side   We seek your forgiveness, Lord. We seek your joy.

Leader   We live in a world of unmended, broken pieces, Lord. Like shattered pieces of pottery are our relationships. Help us to learn the healing power of forgiveness. Help us to seek it from you and to offer it readily to all who seek it from us. May we be unafraid to face you and hold your pardon and your peace close to us.

Pray-er 4   (facing the assembly) You are a God of pardon and peace. We face the brokenness of our world armed with the awesome weapon of forgiveness. Help us, Lord, to be forgiving people. May we be known for our readiness to forgive and our willingness to seek forgiveness. In this we seek to carry out your work and to heal the divisions between us. We pray for your pardon and peace. We pray . . .

Left Side   We seek your pardon, Lord. We seek your peace.

Leader   (holding up the broken and whole pieces of pottery) God of forgiveness, we are like this broken piece of pottery. We sin, we fail to love another. We fail to love you. You make us whole again through the power of your forgiveness. Help us to experience your forgiveness and to be generous in offering to others the forgiveness you have generously offered to us. We pray . . .

All   Amen.
(A sign of peace may be shared.)

15

Learning Peace
A Courageous Response to Violence

Preparing for Prayer

Times for Use
- beginning of school year
- retreat experience, on peacemaking or conflict resolution
- confirmation preparation dealing with reconciliation, love of enemies, and forgiveness
- feast of St. Francis
- World Peace Day

Materials Needed
- bell
- newsprint sheets
- felt-tip marker
- square piece of cloth (3" x 3") for each participant—to be sewn into a quilt

Introduction
Violence today shreds the fabric of social order. Domestic violence is destroying the promise of family stability. Abuse of children and women plague our relationships. Gang violence and violence connected to the drug trade rob the young of life and hope. Internationally, ethnic cleansing has fueled a war of unthinkable atrocities and 1.5 million children are killed in war each year. It is into this landscape of violence that the follower of Christ is asked to follow a different path, a vision full of hope. As Pope John Paul II has reminded us, "The world longs for peace and has a desperate need for peace." This service is a call to renew in the young the power and possibility of living a nonviolent life in a violent world.

Shared Experience

Invite the adolescents to think about the violence they are familiar with. Some examples and their causes may be listed on newsprint: an abusive relationship; violence rooted in prejudice, unjust social structures, the drug culture, wounded pride, and failed relationships.

Ask 2 volunteers to pretend they have a conflict that could lead to violence. Ask them to stand back to back and each to describe what they see physically in front of them: the wall, table, pictures, people. Compare this to the different views of reality that often leads to violence. Ask them whether it would make any sense to start a fight because they have different views. Next, ask them to turn slightly so each can see part of what the other person sees; then to turn a bit more, etc. When one person recognizes what the other is seeing, ring the bell. This ability to see from not only one's own perspective but from the other person's is one of the most important elements in peacemaking. The sound of the bell calls all of us to this experience. Negotiation, taking time out to process anger, bringing in a third party, holding family meetings, trying to reach a consensus, compromise—these are a few of the things we can learn to help us turn conflict into a constructive experience. Conclude by pointing out that the call of Christ is to become peacemakers. This demands that we become familiar with as many ways of creating just and harmonious relationships as we can.

Prayer Service

Focus Prayer

Leader Let us gather as God's holy people to pray that we may help one another to learn the ways of peace. Lord, you have said, "Happy are the peacemakers, for they will be called your children." Keep us close to you in time of conflict. When violence seems the easy way out, be with me to lead me into the way of peace. Help us all to learn peace and not violence, reconciliation and not division.

All Amen.

Through God's Eyes

Leader "Blessed are the peacemakers, for they shall be called the children of God." Today, it is very difficult to be a peacemaker. Violence surrounds us on every side: guns in school, drive-by shootings, attacks on professional athletes, fights over girlfriends and boyfriends, and armed conflicts in places like Bosnia and Haiti. How do you resolve conflict? How vengeful are you? How willing to forgive?

Jesus asked his followers to love their enemies when the enemy was Rome and Roman soldiers marched in the streets of Jerusalem. He told Peter to forgive those who harmed him as often as forgiveness was sought. He included in his command to love even those who consider us enemies. By his death and resurrection he renounced the power of violence in favor of the power of sacrificial love. We will now listen to the words Jesus offers us.

Reading

Reader This passage describes the attitude of the disciple toward those who wish us ill. It describes what life in the spirit means in our relationships. Because we are God's, we love even those who consider us enemies. Because we are invited to share the very life of God, we are invited to embrace all in our love. A reading from the holy gospel according to St. Matthew (5:38–44)

Quiet Time

(A few minutes of silence with appropriate soft music)

	Response
Leader	We gather to be strengthened to do the work peace demands. Let us join in mind and heart that our prayers may rise as one voice to the God of peace.
Pray-er 1	Peace is not possible apart for you, God. You are the author of peace and the source of all just relationships among people. Keep us joined to you through prayer, sacrament, and loving action that we may have hearts ready for peace. We pray, seeking your peace.
Right Side	Prepare our hearts for peace. Keep us close to you and make us your holy people. (A bell rings.)
Pray-er 2	Jesus, you ask us to love our enemies and to do good to those who persecute us. What you ask is impossible without your vision of life and without your faith in the transforming power of love. Keep us close to you, our friend, and give us your vision. We pray, seeking your peace.
Left Side	Prepare our hearts for peace. Keep us close to you and make us your holy people. (A bell rings.)
Pray-er 3	Teacher of peace, we live in a world of violence. Free us from the need to control and dominate one another. Free us from the poison of revenge, from the failure to find acceptance which leads to violence. Free us from the need to hate and support us in our efforts to love. We pray, seeking your peace.
Right Side	Prepare our hearts for peace. Keep us close to you and make us your holy people. (A bell rings.)
Pray-er 4	God of peace, teach us the methods of peace. Motivate us to seek reconciliation and to offer forgiveness when we are wronged. May negotiation, seeking a third way, and taking time to seek consensus become part of the way we respond to conflict. We pray, seeking your peace.
Left Side	Prepare our hearts for peace. Keep us close to you and make us your holy people. (A bell rings.)
Leader	As we seek peace, let us seek justice. May we never compromise when truth would be lost, but may we ever seek ways

to discover truth in our adversaries. And whenever we hear the ring of a bell, may we remember God's call to be people of peace.

All   God, help us prepare our hearts for peace. Keep us close to you and make us your holy people.

(If the participants have pieces of cloth for a quilt, the following conclusion is used.)

Leader   Peace is created from many different people of divergent backgrounds seeking truth. I invite you to come forward to present your patch of cloth which will be sewn into a single peace quilt and hung here as a reminder of our call to peace.

16

Passion
A Way Beyond Sex

Preparing for Prayer

Times for Use
- new school year
- new year of religious education
- class on the connection between sex and love
- prayer service on boredom and the way of wonder
- class on personal transformation

Materials Needed
- looseleaf paper folded in two: on one side at the top of one
  column is the heading: PASSIONATE LIVING; on the other
  side: BORING

Introduction

Adolescence is a time of change characterized by the hormonal activity that leads to new physical growth and new sexual power. Teens face many strong influences at this time that can harm them as they mature. Life will not develop, however, by denying them their newfound capabilities. They are called to live and to live passionately. Jesus is our model in this. He visited friends and broke bread and drank wine with them. He laughed and celebrated human love at their weddings. He cried over their losses and felt pain in body and spirit. He uncovered for them the presence and power of God hidden within human relationships and in human activity. We celebrate Christ's invitation to live each day passionately.

Shared Experience

Pass out the papers. Invite the young people to think of one or two times when they felt full of life, passionate about life. Ask them to jot these down under the column Passionate Living. Next, ask them to think of times they felt lethargic and were bored and to jot these down under Boring. After allowing time for this, ask for some examples. If there is difficulty getting a response, you may mention some experiences. You may write some of the responses on newsprint. Finally, ask them what they think makes life exciting at some times and boring at others. Allow times for responses and write a sample on the newsprint.

Prayer Service

Focus Prayer

Leader   God of life, all of us want to live more fully, aware of the world around us. We want to enter into everyday experiences full of life and energy. We pray to you to show us how we can live more fully, more passionately as Jesus lived.

All   Amen.

Through God's Eyes

Leader   The word "passion" means to suffer as in the passion of Jesus. We may associate the word with sexual relationship, but passion goes beyond sex. It means to live fully or to devote one's full effort to an undertaking, as in playing a sport with passion. It is a quality of character that empowers us to live fully in the moment, to be full of wonder and awe at the ordinary things of life. It is ignited in us by the knowledge that we are created by a loving God, and our lives have deep meaning because of that.

Reading

Reader   This story describes the apostles' awe and wonder at Jesus calming the storm. A reading from the holy gospel according to Luke (8:22–25)

Quiet Time

(A few minutes of silence with appropriate soft music)

Leader   We may think of passion as something we do; we act passionately. But passion is really a way of living each day. It is to see with the eyes of wonder like Helen Keller did. She was blind, as you know, and deaf. A friend went for a walk in the woods and mentioned to Helen that she hadn't seen very much on her walk. Helen paused and asked how someone could walk through the woods without seeing much. Helen lived each day passionately. Boredom is the result of failing to see extraordinary events in the ordinary of each day. Sometimes an accident will shock us out of our complacency, sometimes a sickness or loss of a loved one. But God invites us to realize that each day is a miracle of God's love—which won't be repeated. We pray that we may develop that attitude within ourselves.

Reprinted with permission from *20 More Teen Prayer Services* by Kevin Regan © 1994 Twenty-Third Publications, P.O. Box 180, Mystic, CT 06355. 800-321-0411

	Response
Leader	Our response: Fill us with passion, Lord, fill us with life.
Pray-er 1	Just for this day the sun will shine and Earth will come alive for us. We pray that we may live fully present to the wonder of this day . . .
All	Fill us with passion, Lord, fill us with life.
Pray-er 2	Just for this day the flowers will bloom, the trees will offer us shade, and the fresh air will fill our lungs. We pray that we may live fully present to the wonder of this day . . .
All	Fill us with passion, Lord, fill us with life.
Pray-er 3	Just for this day we will have friends to be with us, people who love us. We pray we may live fully present to the wonder of this day . . .
All	Fill us with passion, Lord, fill us with life.
Pray-er 4	Just for today I can laugh and sing and dance and love. We pray we may live fully present to the wonder of this day . . .
All	Fill us with passion, Lord, fill us with life.
Pray-er 5	Just for today I am given the opportunity to know I am alive, that God loves me and Jesus walks with me as he walked with his friends in Jerusalem. We pray we may live fully present to the wonders of this day . . .
All	Fill us with passion, Lord, fill us with life.
Leader	Lord Jesus, you used birds and fish and wheat as subjects of your stories. You embraced small children and made bread a sacrament of your presence. Help us to overcome boredom by becoming involed in everything we say and do. We pray to you, the God of all passion.
All	Lord, help us to walk with you this year. Allow our hearts to be full of love and our minds full of wonder. Help us to look out at your world with with the eyes of love, with your eyes, our brother, our Lord, and friend. Amen.

17

Being With the Poor
The Way of Justice

Preparing for Prayer

Times for Use
• school community service programs
• service projects for confirmation preparation
• Christian Service Retreat
• Thanksgiving Day
• feast of Martin de Porres
• Pentecost

Materials Needed
• salt
• water
• lectern
• newsprint sheets
• felt-tip markers
• pins
• 4"x4" pieces of paper

Introduction
More and more people are living in poverty in this country amid wide areas of wealth and comfortable living. According to the Children's Defense Fund, the number of Americans living in poverty in 1992 was over 36 million. Unemployment, underemployment, lack of job training, poor schooling, addictions, the deinstitutionalization of the mentally ill, teenage pregnancy are some of the many factors contributing to poverty. For some, such as Native Americans, policies forcing assimilation into the mainstream or attempting extermination have contributed to the destruction of a culture while creating poverty among a once self-sufficient people.

Although the causes vary, the plight of the poor calls out for a response from the followers of Christ. In a culture that too often blames the victim, the church stands as a sign of contradiction true to Jesus who was born poor and was known simply as the carpenter's son. To a people encouraged to "climb the ladder to success," Jesus comes down the ladder of godliness, emptying himself to embrace the poverty of humanity. This service is meant to challenge those perspectives that ask us to accept poverty as normal. It is meant as a support to become more identified with the needs of God's poor.

Shared Experience

Ask the participants what images come to mind when they think of poverty. Write these on the newsprint, paying special attention to those who have experienced what it means to be poor. Next, invite volunteers to come forward to be part of a conference to root out the causes of poverty. Give each participant a folded piece of paper and a pin. On the outside of the paper write a designation such as, I am from Laos. On the inside write information such as as, I am a male, I am hungry, I make 25 cents a day. Participants pin on their name tag, with the designation alone showing. Other possibilities are: I am a Native American, I am from Wounded Knee, South Dakota, the poorest place in the U.S. Or, I am from Haiti, I am ten years old, I am hungry, baseballs are made in my country, the poorest in the Western hemisphere. Or, I am a white American, I own three cars and make $200,000 a year. Add as many designations as you need for each conference participant to have one.

Next, let the "poor" people sit on the floor to work at the causes of poverty while the "rich" sit at a table set with dishes and plenty of food such as cake, cookies, soda—and a waiter. The rich may talk to the poor, but the poor may not talk to the rich. If they try, police designated by their name tags will put the poor in jail. This is a section of floor space formed with chairs. After a period of time, ask each to read the description of who they are on the inside of the papers. Ask what each felt like and allow the group to discuss what issues arose or what insights were gained.

Prayer Service

Focus Prayer

Leader   We are gathered together to try to understand the perspective of the poor and to support one another in seeking to stand with the poor. God of the poor, we ask you to help us to search for justice, to help the oppressed, to be just to the orphan and to plead for the widow. Help us to be your people, God of the poor.

All   Help us to be your people, God of the poor.

Leader   Often we blame the poor for their poverty. We cut ourselves off from one another and build walls of fear and hate. Help us to realize that what happens to one of us affects us all. Help us to be united in your love for all people. Help us to be your people, God of the poor.

All   Help us to be your people, God of the poor. Amen.

Through God's Eyes

Leader   Do you ever wonder how God views the huge inequalities in our world? The world's population of over 5.5 billion people is characterized by the divisions between rich and poor. Many of the rich live in countries that have traditionally been Christian. How can this be? How can we claim allegiance to Christ and at the same time seek after wealth and comfort while so many of our neighbors are perishing in poverty? It is the responsibility of the Christian to work to free the poor from oppression. But to seek our own security or to claim a right to accumulating property and wealth because "I earned it" is to mock the gospel and the person of Christ. What we may seek for our own is limited by the just demands of our sisters and brothers who have much less of this world's goods.

Many are accustomed to sacrificing food in order to lose weight, or sacrificing a night's sleep in order to comfort a troubled friend. In the same way, God calls us to sacrifice those material things that are a hindrance to love of God and neighbor, in order to be free to love all people and to give of ourselves for the sake of God's love, God's reign. Let us reflect together on God's word to us.

Reprinted with permission from 20 More Teen Prayer Services by Kevin Regan
© 1994 Twenty-Third Publications, P.O. Box 180, Mystic, CT 06355. 800-321-0411

	Reading
Reader	This reading describes the role of the disciple to live in such a way that people are led to praise God. A reading from the holy gospel according to St. Matthew (5:13–16)

Quiet Time
(A few minutes of silence with appropriate soft music)

	Response
Leader	(holding the salt high) We are the salt of Earth.
Right Side	We are the salt of Earth.
Leader	(holding the candle high) We are the light of the world.
Left Side	We are the light of the world.
Leader	(holding both the salt and candle) We are salt. We are light. Our light must shine in the sight of all.
Right Side	We are salt. We are light. Our light must shine in the sight of all.
Leader	The Lord hears the cry of the poor.
Left Side	The Lord hears the cry of the poor.
Leader	God of the poor, God of justice, hear our prayers for conversion. May we place your love and love for our neighbor before the accumulation of material wealth or worldly ambition. Help us to walk with the poor as a friend and to seek the justice that the prophets acclaim as the surest sign of your presence. We all pray.
All	Help us to walk with the poor. Help us to be just. Amen.
Leader	(Give each person a small pinch of salt or a candle with appropriate music playing.) You are the salt of the earth (or, You are the light of the world).
All	I will be light to God's poor (or, I will be salt for God's poor). Amen.

18

Human Labor
More Than Making Money

Preparing for Prayer

Times for Use
- career days
- retreat on vocation and planning for the future
- confirmation preparation, on being a witness
- Labor Day
- St. Joseph the Worker

Materials Needed
- hammer
- saw
- needle and thread
- notebook and pen
- diaper
- band aid (this and all the above are to be displayed)
- felt-tip markers
- newsprint with the heading, We Can Build a Better World

Introduction
Many adolescents have jobs after school. As they approach high school graduation, many begin to think about careers, what they would like to do in the future. The culture tells them the purpose of human labor is to make money. Earning a fair living is one aspect of human labor, of course, but to reduce labor to making money is to dehumanize the laborer. Labor not only allows us to support ourselves and our families, but allows us to develop our talents and influence the world. The worker is united to others in service and collaborates to develop creation for the benefit of all. Indeed, by offering his or her labor to God, the worker is associated with the saving work of Christ. This is the gift we celebrate in this service.

Shared Experience

Leader	(Call attention to the tools on display and their related occupations.) In order to focus our attention on work, let us listen to a panel discussing the reasons people work.
Speaker	Tonight we are going to uncover some of the reasons people are motivated to work. Panelist number 1, why do you work?
Panelist 1	I work with my mind in order to get good grades to go to college. I want to get a good job and a college education seems necessary. I spend a lot of time on school work. I believe it is worth it.
Speaker	Panelist number 2, what about you?
Panelist 2	I work both in school and after school. I work in a nursing home talking to the people there. Many of them are lonely and I hope some day to be a social worker and give my time and talents to caring for lonely people.
Speaker	Panelist number 3, what motivates you to work?
Panelist 3	I have two jobs after school now. I work a night shift in a jewelry factory and afternoons in a pizza parlor. I work to make money. Money buys the things I want, and if I can make enough of it in the future, it will bring me power and happiness.
Speaker	Now I ask our final panelist, why do you work?
Panelist 4	I work helping to prepare meals in a local hospital. I want to be a chef and this gives me a way to slowly develop my talent. But I also get a chance to talk with the sick and even some dying people. This has taught me that relationships are more important than money, and it has helped me to value living each day fully, one day at a time.

Prayer Service

Focus Prayer

Leader   God, all of us work in order to make a living. Help us to gain a greater understanding of human labor. You blessed all human labor by working as a carpenter's son and as a teacher. Help us as we use our talents to improve conditions in the world today. We to pray to the Lord.

All   Amen.

Through God's Eyes

Leader   We will listen together to God's word, which reminds us that our work is to include in some way those in need, that we show our love for God by our love for others—all others.

Reading

(The reading may be done in two parts, with a narrator and God in dialogue.)

Reader   The parable of the last judgment illustrates that love of neighbor is the end of all human endeavors. Realizing that we are in the presence of God, we will listen to God's word from the holy gospel according to Matthew (25:31–46)

Quiet Time

(A few minutes of silence with appropriate soft music)

Leader   I ask you to remember the words of Jesus. Each of us has been given gifts that we will use in our work to make a living. But no matter what work we do, all of our labor is to build God's reign on Earth. This means that as we work to make a living we also develop our talents in a positive way and better the lives of our sisters and brothers in the human family. Through us and our labor God continues the work of Christ to love and heal the human family.

Response

Leader   Let us pray to God that we may use our talents well and labor in ways that will build up the human family and God's church.

Girl   God, the creator of the world, has made us to labor so that we may develop our talents and build up the human family. In gratitude, let us pray to the Lord.

Reprinted with permission from *20 More Teen Prayer Services* by Kevin Regan © 1994 Twenty-Third Publications, P.O. Box 180, Mystic, CT 06355. 800-321-0411

All	Creator God, we thank you for making us co-creators with you in working to build a more human world for all.
Boy	Jesus, you praised your father and loved your brothers and sisters by the work you did with your hands. You were known as the carpenter's son. You also preached the word of God's love to the people of your day. Help us to choose careers in which we can use our gifts to glorify God and bring happiness and joy to others. We pray to the Lord.
All	Help us, Jesus, our friend, to work joyfully as a way to love others and be joined with you.
Girl	St. Joseph, you provided for your family and developed your own skills through your labor. Help us to work diligently to develop our talents and place them at the service of God and God's people. We pray this in God's name.
All	Amen.
Leader	Go with God's blessing. May you work hard and well for the glory of God. May you help to develop the world's resources responsibly. May you work to improve the conditions of human beings everywhere.

19

Transformed by God
Becoming a Eucharistic People

Preparing for Prayer

Times for Use
• retreat day, on church or eucharist
• confirmation preparation, on eucharist, or thanksgiving
• Corpus Christi
• Holy Thursday

Materials Needed
• loaf of bread
• cup of wine
• candle
• empty chair
• signs reading: Power, Money, Popularity, Pleasure, Success, Comfort

Introduction
Part of the American dream is material, economic well-being. Indeed, this value has dominated the culture in many ways. Yet, the promised fulfillment seems missing since violence, drugs, sexual permissiveness, and boredom are pervasive among the young and society at large. Jesus invites us to a life of service characterized by gratitude and joy in doing the work of God. The eucharist stands as the great counter-cultural sign of our age. Through Jesus we have a window to God's view of the purpose of life: loving service of others, suffering with and for the other, repentance, humility, and joyous gratitude in the presence of God. Only as we are transformed by God's grace can we move away from the influence of our culture and into the reign of God. This service celebrates faith in God's transforming power and in the gift of the eucharist to transform us into God's holy people.

Shared Experience

Have the candle lit in the front center of the assembly with the bread and wine on either side of a table or altar and an empty chair in front of the table or altar.) Invite the participants to look at the signs: Power, Money, Popularity, Pleasure, Success, Comfort. Ask them to jot down which of these are important to them. Ask if there are other values not listed that are important to them. Allow time to discuss this.

Leader   Many of society's values fall short in delivering what they promise. They often focus on our physical wants and needs, while ignoring our deeper needs for intimacy, a meaningful life, loving relationships, and helping others in need. Jesus offers us a more complete vision of life. We are a people with a special calling: to manifest love in our homes, in school, on the athletic field, in our places of work. By his presence, Jesus helps us bring the love of God into every aspect of daily life. The bread and wine you see before you are the great signs that love is more powerful than hate, life more powerful than the forces of sin and death. Jesus is with us today in the sacrament of love as a light, and so the candle. Look at the empty chair and imagine it is Jesus' chair. Ask whether you could sit in it and carry on his work and live his values in today's world. Jot down a few of the values of Jesus.

Prayer Service

Focus Prayer

Leader   God, your son Jesus lived and died out of love for us. He left us a sign of his presence and his love in the eucharist. We pray that we may meet him in this sacrament and we may become your holy people doing your will on Earth. Let us pray.

All   Amen.

Through God's Eyes

Leader   There are many stories of courage and suffering about the actions taken to save Jews from Hitler's policies of extermination in World War II. One story is told of a whole village in southern France that organized its "underground" to save Jewish children from deportation to the death camps. At risk of life, the people led by André Trocmé hid the children and their families from the Nazis and smuggled them out of France to safety. They took seriously Jesus' command to love others and to be a eucharistic people.

Whenever we eat the body of the Lord, we renew our dedication to try to love one another as God loves us. The eucharist transforms us from being self-centered to being other-centered and God-centered. We are empowered to love and serve others because we are so filled with God's love for us. We are filled with thanksgiving because we know that God loves us absolutely. All about us are the signs of God's love. (Mention Jean Vanier, Mother Teresa, or local communities who are eucharist for one another.) We will listen now to a reading that tells of Jesus' eucharistic love and invitation to us to live out of that love.

Reading

Reader   The reading describes the institution of the eucharist. A reading from the first letter of St. Paul to the Corinthians (11:23–25)

Quiet Time

(A few minutes of silence with appropriate soft music)

Response

(Have the participants assembled in a semi-circle around the empty chair, and a table or altar with bread and wine and the candle on it.)

Reprinted with permission from *20 More Teen Prayer Services* by Kevin Regan
© 1994 Twenty-Third Publications, P.O. Box 180, Mystic, CT 06355. 800-321-0411

Leader	Like bread, love is food that nourishes God's people. Before we can sit in Jesus' chair, we must eat of the bread so we can bring his love to one another. Who will eat this bread? Who will put on Christ by sitting in this chair, a symbol of his love?
	(Pray-er 1 comes forward, eats of the bread, and sits in the chair. The assembly prays one moment in silence. Pray-er 1 stands and prays.)
Pray-er 1	Lord Jesus, I eat this bread as a sign that I seek to be united with you and become food for others. I sit in this chair as a sign of my desire to bring you into the empty places of our world. Please join me in prayer.
All	We do this, Lord, in memory of you.
	(Repeat this process for as many times as seems appropriate.)
Leader	God, this bread and wine (holding them high) become in the liturgy of the eucharist the body and blood of Christ. Help us to celebrate this sacrament often. And after being fed, transform us into your holy people. Help us to fill all the empty places and empty hearts that seek the comfort and courage of Christ in today's world. We pray . . .
All	Let it be done to us, Lord, according to your will. Amen.

20

Fire in the Belly
The Dark Night of Adolescence

Preparing for Prayer

Times for Use
• youth retreat
• confirmation preparation, on life in the Spirit
• celebration of the struggles and triumphs of adolescents today

Materials Needed
• large candle
• small pieces of paper
• pencils
• an offering plate

Introduction
Some may wonder at the association of fire and a dark night. But mystics of every age have associated these seemingly contradictory symbols with the spiritual journey we all have to take. The "dark night" is a symbol for troubled times, for feeling depressed or lost. The "fire" is the spark or charge within us that lightens our way and leads to the creation of new art forms or the solution of social problems, giving life to ideas and ideals. But the fire of God within and the heart longing to be consumed by that fire are gifts we receive. We must wait in emptiness and hope until God's fire enkindles our hearts.

Adolescence is a time marked by rapid change. It is a passage out of the safe harbor of childhood into the stormy seas of adult responsibility. It is a period of transcendence, of uncertainty. During this time, idealism plays on the same field with frustration, and unbounded involvement dances on the same floor with fearful withdrawal. Something new and powerful is alive within. There is an insatiable longing that tells the young there is more.

Adolescence must be encountered alone. All is opaque, except the questions: Am I normal? Where am I going? Will I ever get there? Yet as most of the light is caught in the darkest part of the negative, the darkness of not knowing, of feeling unattached, leads to a faith in the process of growing, in the knowledge others have made it, in the hope that one is experiencing the birth of someone new. One learns that God is in the darkness as well as the light. This service is to recognize and reverence the struggle and transcendence that are part of adolescence.

Shared Experience

Have the room in diminished light except for a few lights and the candle. Pass out a pencil and piece of paper to each participant. Call attention to the darkness and ask them to think of moments in their lives when things seemed dark, without hope. Ask them to write down one of these. Next, ask them to think of a time after this experience when they felt that all was well. Ask them to try to identify anything in their moment of darkness that might have led them to believe they would eventually be all right, perhaps knowing a friend would be there, or that God would take care of them, or knowing they had support from their parents. Ask them to write these down on the reverse side of the paper. Explain that each person goes through periods of darkness when life seems to be difficult, unbending, leading nowhere. Most often the greatest growth takes place only by passing through some difficulty or challenge. In times of darkness, we can learn to live by a deeper standard than what is easy and available. We can learn to live by faith.

Prayer Service

Focus Prayer

Leader   We gather as one family with many members. Although we are different in many ways, we are united in the knowledge that all of us pass through times of darkness in order to reach a new level of life. We pray for one another that we may recognize God's presence in the darkness as well as in moments of light. Let us pray.

All   Amen.

Through God's Eyes

Leader   Some of you may know the Greek myth of Sisyphus. Sisyphus was condemned to roll a large rock up a mountain. Just as he is about to reach the top, the rock rolls back down and he must begin all over again. No doubt there are times when we feel like Sisyphus. We try and try, but we feel like we are always back at the beginning. Sometimes we know there is more to life than the routine of school, work, and social events, but we are in the dark when trying to discover the real meaning of life. We feel excited at times by the new powers we are discovering within ourselves, but we can't quite harness those powers or feel as accomplished and genuine as we would like. But all of us experience these moments and with patience and trust in God, ourselves, and others and in the dynamism of life, we will transcend them and become a person with wonderful powers to think and love and create. This is like a passing from death to a new life, and Jesus' death and resurrection are a truer example of what happens than the myth of Sisyphus. Let us listen to a description of Jesus' dark night.

Reading

Reader   The passages tell of the crucifixion and death of Jesus. A reading from the holy gospel according to St. Mark (15:22–27, 33–39)

(After a pause the following is read:) This passage tells of the resurrection. A reading from the holy gospel according to St. Mark (16:1–8)

Quiet Time
(A few minutes of silence with appropriate soft music)

Reprinted with permission from *20 More Teen Prayer Services* by Kevin Regan
© 1994 Twenty-Third Publications, P.O. Box 180, Mystic, CT 06355. 800-321-0411

Response

(In diminished light, have a large candle at the front of the assembly.)

Leader   We have reflected on our dark nights and the dark night of Jesus. We believe that God is in the darkness as well as the light. We believe with the monk and poet Thomas Merton that the root of Christian love is not our will to love but the faith that God loves us. We pray for that faith when all seems dark.

Pray-er 1   When all seems lost around us and within, we pray.

Right Side   When all seems lost, we pray for the faith to realize that God loves us.

Pray-er 2   When like Jesus we feel empty and abandoned and all is dark, we pray.

Left Side   When like Jesus we feel empty and abandoned and all seems dark, we pray for the faith to realize that God loves us.

Pray-er 3   When like Jesus we are asked to carry our cross, and all seems without hope, we pray.

Right Side   When like Jesus we are asked to carry our cross, and all seems without hope, we pray for the faith to realize that God loves us.

Pray-er 4   When we are lost and feel life pulling us in a million directions, we pray for faith to hear the call of God and the courage to act responsibly to answer that call.

Left Side   When we are lost and feel life pulling us in a million directions, we pray for faith to hear the call of God and the courage to act responsibly to answer that call.

Pray-er 5   Jesus, our darkness and our light, in all of our dark nights help us to keep our eyes fixed on you. Let your word be a light to guide us and may your resurrection be our source of hope that we too shall rise to splendid new life.

All   Jesus, our darkness and our light, in all of our dark nights help us to keep our eyes fixed on you. May your word be a light to guide us, and may your resurrection be our source of hope that we too will rise to splendid new life. Amen.

(The leader may invite the participants to present their papers, which are then burned in a metal pot, using the candle that was lit to ignite the fire.)

Leader   May you come out of darkness into lasting light.

All   Amen.

Of Related Interest...

Teen Prayer Services
20 Themes for Reflection
Kevin Regan
Services focus on issues important to teens. Great for retreats, special sessions and regular classes.

ISBN: 0-89622-520-8, 80 pp, $9.95

Seasonal Prayer Services for Teenagers
Greg Dues
These 16 prayer services help teenagers understand the themes found in the holidays of the seasons, the church year and the civic year.

ISBN: 0-89622-473-2, 80 pp, $9.95

Searching for Faith
Prayer Experiences for Teen Assemblies and Retreats
Greg Dues
The 20 prayer experiences found here are straightforward, with a minimum amount of preparation time needed.

ISBN: 0-89622-561-5, 96 pp, $9.95

Quicksilvers
Ministering with Junior High Youth
Carole Goodwin
Deals with the unique developmental characteristics, personal needs, crisis issues and faith concerns of young adolescents.

ISBN: 0-89622-519-4, 96 pp, $7.95

Available at religious bookstores or from

TWENTY-THIRD PUBLICATIONS
P.O. Box 180 • Mystic, CT 06355

1-800-321-0411